A History of the House of Lords

Lord Longford

SUTTON PUBLISHING

First published in 1988 by William Collins Sons and Co Ltd

This edition published in 1999 by Sutton Publishing Limited
Phoenix Mill · Thrupp · Stroud · Gloucestershire GL5 2BU

A catalogue record for this book is available from the British
Library

ISBN 0 7509 2191 9

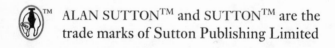 ALAN SUTTON™ and SUTTON™ are the
trade marks of Sutton Publishing Limited

Printed and bound in Great Britain by
Biddles Limited, Guildford, Surrey.

Contents

PREFACE TO 1999 EDITION

This book was published eleven years ago. Since then the composition of the House of Lords has changed somewhat but not drastically. Some information about the present composition of the House of Lords follows.

Analysis of composition – 1 December 1998

By Party Strength

Party	Life Peers	Hereditary Peers of first creation	by succession	Lords Spiritual	Total
Conservative	173	4	298		475
Labour	158	1	17		176
Liberal Democrats	45	0	24		69
Cross Bench	120	4	198		322
Other	9	0	89	26	124
	505	9	626	26	1166

NB: Excludes peers without Writs of Summons (68) or on leave of absence

By Type

Archbishops and Bishops		26
Hereditary Peers (by succession)	(16 women)	750
Hereditary Peers (of first creation)		9
Life Peers under the Appellate Jurisdiction Act 1876		28
Life Peers under the Life Peerages Act 1958	(87 women)	484
Total including:		1297
Lords without Writs of Summons	(2 minors, 68 Hereditary)	68
Peers on leave of absence	(7 life and 56 hereditary)	63

By Rank

Prince (of Blood Royal)		1
Archbishops		2
Dukes and Dukes of Blood Royal	25 & 3	28
Marquesses		34
Earls and Countesses	169 & 5	174
Viscounts		103
Bishops		24
Barons/Lords and Baronesses and Ladies	833 & 95 & 3	931
Total		1297

For me, a member for 53 years, and I suspect for most old-timers, the House is still very much the same place. It still performs two essential, if overlapping, functions. One, the expert revision of legislation passed from the House of Commons or discussion of similar legislation where it starts in the Lords. Two, a vital long-term influence on British life and policy. I have played no great part in the first process where lawyers have been in their element.

I have, however, during ten years in government and 43 on the backbenches made innumerable speeches and opened many debates on social questions in particular. I cannot help mentioning that I have proposed a number of Motions on subjects not previously raised in my recollection in that way in the House. Among them I recall universities, the youth service, children's homes, hospices for the dying, prisons, the probation service, pornography, victims of crime and voluntary action.

I had the great honour of carrying what I shall always call The Alf Morris Bill on disablement through the Lords. In these respects life for myself and the other active members does not alter over time except that our speeches are very much shorter. When I was a Minister after the war Front Bench speeches were quite often almost an hour in length. Now they occupy about half that time and backbenchers are well advised to keep under ten minutes. No one who doubts the idealism of the House of Lords should be unaware of a recent debate on charities when 28 peers (2 bishops, 14 hereditary peers, 12 life peers) took part, all doing fine work in that area.

What, however, has changed dramatically in the last ten years is the situation in which the House finds itself. For the first time in my half century there a grave threat hangs over it and there is a real threat of it being transformed from outside in the next year or two. For many years the Labour Party was committed in the abstract to the abolition of the House of Lords. But even when they had a large majority from 1945 to 1951 no one in the House took the threat very seriously. When I was Leader of the House from 1964 to 1968 I brought forward compromise proposals which would have allowed hereditary peers to remain members and speak but not vote. The proposals were accepted by leaders of the main parties in both Houses. They were sabotaged by a strange cross-bench and back-bench coalition in the House of Commons. But the issue died away without much further attention.

In 1987, as mentioned at the end of the present book, the Labour Party for the first time made no reference to reform of the Lords. But, at the last election, the Labour manifesto made clear that if Labour were returned to power they would set to work in earnest to remove the hereditary peerage in the House. It is understood, at the time of writing (8 January 1999) that the government will introduce at once in the new session a Bill to dispose of the hereditary peers. What are the reasons for this remarkable change of front? Only the leaders of the parties can speak with authority, but for my part I distinguish two. I pass over any suggestion that the behaviour of the Lords since the Labour government came in has been responsible for any change of attitude. Most obviously the overwhelming victory of the party and their huge majority in the House of Commons make it certain that, in the end, their will must prevail. But, as pointed out above, the commitment was there before the result of the election was known. The conclusion must I would think have been reached, that the House of Lords, collectively speaking, was unpopular and drastic reform of it would go down well with the public.

I hesitate to challenge this verdict. Speaking for myself I have not found that being a Lord lost one friends. In my experience invitations to the House whether or not accompanied by me are eagerly snapped up. The yearning for membership seems as great as ever. Sir Isaiah Berlin is known to have declined the honour. So has Jack Jones, the great Transport & General Workers' leader. It is understood that Michael Foot would also decline. No doubt there are others with the same attitude. But, by and large, there are far more aspiring candidates than can be accommodated.

'This', said Lord Salisbury, the grandfather of the Leader of the Opposition in the House on a famous occasion, 'is a House of Parliament not a club'. He said to a Labour peer who was criticised for attacking Lord Salisbury because the latter had not disclosed a connection with Rhodesia. The Labour peer told it to me with tears in his eyes. But many members, old and young, feel it is the best club in the world. Nevertheless in voting terms to attack the Lords seems to be good business.

What then of the immediate future? Only two broad possibilities present themselves. Either the hereditary peers will disappear from the scene – kicking and squealing perhaps – without trace; or there will be some compromise to minimise the painful parting. On the face of it the first possibility is the more likely. The Lords can hold up legislation for a year but after that they can be ignored and the hereditaries could be removed whatever the protest. On the other hand, in that year, the House of Lords – or the majority of it – which objects to their brutal exclusion could make themselves a thorough nuisance to the government. It has always seemed possible that some compromise will be reached.

Every Tom, Dick and Harry seems to have his own idea as to what should be done with the Lords. For my part the only two compromises that seem conceivable are – one, the original 'two-writ' plan referred to earlier under which hereditary peers would come and speak but not vote; two, some deal with the representatives of the hereditary peers under which a number of them reappeared as life peers. The second has always seemed much more likely than the first. Whatever happens some of the leading 'hereditaries' are likely to receive life peerages.

At the time of writing it seems more than likely that the deal will go through which was come to between the government and Lord Cranborne, then leader of the Opposition Peers. Under this deal 91 hereditary peers would survive until the second stage of reform. What of the merits of the issue? For myself, as a member of the Labour Party for over 60 years I have to accept the democratic view that in principle no one should be entitled, because of his ancestry, to an automatic place in the British legislature. No one, if one was building a new state, would include the hereditary element in the legislature. But national institutions are not built anew. Tradition played its part even if it be an indefinable element. No one who has been a member of the House of Lords for 50 years will feel that it will benefit from a revolutionary break from its past.

Today our debates are, in my opinion rightly, described as of superior intellectual quality to those of the House of Commons. Rightly or wrongly we believe that in their own fashion they cannot be matched elsewhere in the world. It is true no doubt that this can be attributed reasonably enough to the exceptional qualifications of the life peers; 26 bishops, 28 law lords or former law lords, 15 or so professors, many eminent doctors and former government servants, top business and trades union leaders and a wide selection of former Cabinet Ministers, including 2 Prime Ministers. There are individual hereditary peers – Earl Russell, Lord Cranborne (accelerated into the house), former Leader of the House, now Leader of the Opposition, Lord Carrington, Lord Windlesham, Lord Elton, Lord Hylton and Lord Shepherd to name only a few who played leading parts in the major debate. Half the leaders of the House in my time have been hereditary peers. The leaders from the life peers have been excellent, but no one would claim that the hereditary leaders have been in any way inferior. But I myself go deeper when I think of what the hereditary peerage has meant to the House of Lords. Visitors to the House from this country and other parts of the world have told me again and again how struck they are by the good manners, civilised style and inherent decency of our discussions. And no one can seriously doubt that this is an expression of a long tradition. The Christian influences in the House, to which the hereditary peers have made notable contribution have been particularly strong. I myself for example attend prayer groups presided by hereditary peers.

I do not want readers of this book to look on me as putting a particular case for a future second chamber. One thing is certain: drastic reform is coming and must come. But it will be tragic if all that is most valuable in the old House is abandoned in the new one.

ACKNOWLEDGEMENTS

My first acknowledgement must be to Elizabeth for her help in all things as always. In her *Prelude* she captures a moment in the life of the House in a manner far beyond my powers.

My gratitude goes next to Mr David Jones, Deputy Librarian, and the staff of the House of Lords library. His far-reaching knowledge and theirs have only been matched by an untiring readiness to help me, however actively he and they were engaged in other services to the House. This book would never have been achieved without them.

I am much indebted also to Lord Henderson of Brompton, former Clerk of the Parliaments, to Sir John Sainty, the present Clerk, to Mr Michael Wheeler-Booth, Clerk Assistant, and all members of their staff. I take the opportunity of thanking Air Chief Marshal Sir John Gingell GBE KCB, Gentleman Usher of the Black Rod, Brigadier David M Stileman OBE, Yeoman Usher of the Black Rod, and all members of the staff of the House of Lords in the widest sense for their courtesy and helpfulness over so many years. This is at least one sentence in the present book which will be echoed by all members of the House.

Gwen Keeble as always has been my closest ally. For their work on the manuscript I must also thank Barbara Winch, an old and Kitty Champman, a more recent friend. My sincere thanks also go to Jane Davies, so zealous and efficient, and the staff of the St. Stephen's secretariat.

I have received much encouragement from many friends and acquaintances. I must at least mention Lord Ampthill, Lord Greenhill, Lord Rankeillour and Lord Killearn; among my labour colleagues Lord Stallard, 'the hope of the homeless', Lord Parry, a true embodiment of Welsh culture, and Lord Blease, the staunch representative of reconciliation in Northern Ireland. I must thank also Matthew Oliver with whom I have worked in various capacities.

I have been fortunate in having the expert assistance on the seventeenth century of my daughter Antonia Fraser (Lady Antonia Pinter), in having Stuart Proffitt of Collins as my editor, and in having Sara Waters, the daughter of one of our oldest friends, to assemble the pictures.

PRELUDE

by Elizabeth Longford

The solemn Introduction of a new peer into the House of Lords is in a sense the beginning and end of its history. If there were no more creations and introductions there could in time be no more House of Lords. Life peers would inevitably die off, hereditary lines might eventually die out. The ceremony of Introduction itself contains many layers of history: political, religious and royal layers; not to mention certain inexplicable layers of meaning that are now lost in the past. Curiosities, anomalies and contradictions are woven into its tissue. It is also full of moving and impressive symbolism. I have therefore chosen to give my own brief impression of an actual Introduction, as prelude to this fascinating, far-ranging story.

It is not my first impression. I have been present in the Peeresses' Gallery to witness the Introduction first of my husband in 1945, then of friends through the years. Not too long ago there was Lord Montgomery, followed by Lord Attlee; quite recently Lady Warnock and Lord Jay, and now, 42 years from 1945, I am watching Baron St. John of Fawsley being introduced.

First impressions did not exactly change with the passage of so much time; rather they were sharpened and expanded by the need to observe and remember so that afterwards I could question and understand. (Notebooks and pencils are not admitted to the Peeresses' Gallery.)

To enter the debating or 'Parliament Chamber', as it is properly called, is to find oneself in an Aladdin's Cave. But it is a brilliantly lit cave located, apparently, in the heart of medieval England. Every intricate piece of wood-carving, every sculptured stone, every polished oak table, all the linenfold panelling, all the bishops' scutcheons in the tall stained-glass windows are seemingly Gothic. The light from the standing brass chandeliers, each with six lamps, is so dazzling that it is almost impossible to decide whether the Gothic lettering on the painted and gilded ceiling is Latin or English; but one assumes it must be Latin, for we are surely in a parliament Chamber of the fourteenth or fifteenth century – and one happily gives up trying to decipher it.

Medieval also are the themes of the six great frescoes in the arched recesses at the north and south ends of the Chamber. There is time, before the Introduction begins, to make out knights in armour, ladies in embroidered robes with circlets of gold on their flowing hair, a harpist, a gauntlet thrown down on a step, a bishop's mitre on another step, a plumed hat on a third. A king clothed only in a loin-cloth is being baptised by an archbishop – that must be pre-medieval – and two female figures seem to be allegorical – one holding a sword, the other the scales of justice. In fact one knows that the medieval Palace of Westminster was swept by fire on 16 October 1834 – the very same date, though 153 years earlier, that a hurricane swept away so many of England's trees. A glorious phoenix, more Gothic than the Gothic, has risen from its ashes.

The illusion is sustained as the whispering and footfalls cease and the ceremony of Introduction begins. The ornate doors at the northern end of the Chamber open and the figure of Black Rod appears. He is an officer of the Order of the Garter, founded by Edward III, and carries a black rod in his black gloved right hand and wears a white satin bow on each shoulder of his black tail coat; he is undoubtedly the smartest figure in the House. Behind him comes Garter King of Arms in a splendid tabard of red, blue and gold with the arms of England, Scotland, Ireland and Wales; there are scarlet satin bows on his shoulders. In his right hand is his silver-gilt sceptre of office, in his left the new peer's patent of creation on a vellum scroll. Then follow in single file behind Garter the new peer himself supported by two peers of his own rank, the junior in front of him, the senior behind. All three wear their scarlet and ermine parliamentary robes. In this case the two supporters or sponsors must be barons, and in fact the senior is Baron Home, the junior Baron Charteris.

There is room for a query here. Surely this senior supporter was the *Earl* of Home before he renounced his title, quitting the Lords to rule the Commons as Alec Douglas-Home, Prime Minister? True; but a peer who has renounced returns, if at all, at the bottom of the ladder. As Churchill once joked in another context, 'you can rat but not re-rat' – at least not without paying the penalty. The same sort of thing has happened to Lord Hailsham: originally a *Viscount*, he left the Lords to become Quintin Hogg MP and returned to be Lord Chancellor as *Baron* Hailsham. Note that this anomalous requirement is not sanctified by time but was recently invented to deal with the new right to renounce. However, a historical anomaly can be discovered in the office of Lord Chancellor itself. Though called by the title of *Lord*, the Chancellor is not necessarily a Member of the Peerage; witness *Sir* Thomas More, Lord Chancellor in the sixteenth century. There is a historic reason for this apparent contradiction. The Lord Chancellor, sitting as he does on the Woolsack, is not part of the House of Peers but belongs to the area of the Throne immediately behind him. In theory there is nothing to stop him being a plain Mister.

Meanwhile our three peers have reached the Bar of the House (the ornamental brass barrier behind which MPs and younger sons of peers may stand to listen), each carrying his black cocked hat in his left hand, the new Peer with his Writ of Summons in his right. All three bow. I used to think they were bowing to the Lord Chancellor, but on learning that they were bowing to the 'Cloth of Estate', I made the further mistake of imagining that the Cloth of Estate was the Throne itself. For there it stood on the shining dais with a fitted cover of red cloth piped in yellow. Not so. The Cloth of Estate marks the position which the Sovereign, if present, would occupy, beneath the carved canopy glittering above the Throne. Then why 'cloth'? Because in the old days the sovereign carried the canopy around with him and it was indeed woven of rich cloth that could be folded for transport.

We have left the three peers advancing up the 'temporal', or west, side of the House. Why 'temporal'? Because the bishops or 'Lords Spiritual' sit on the east side of the Chamber, making it 'spiritual'. I was amused to note that this arrangement has the effect of making the government 'spiritual' and the Opposition 'temporal', since they sit facing each other on the east and west sides of the House respectively.

Our three peers bow again as they reach the Table (where the clerks sit) and yet again when they process to the Judges' Woolsacks (where the judges sit at the State Opening of parliament). Then the new peer approaches *the* Woolsack, where the Lord Chancellor is awaiting him in white wig, black tricorne hat, black breeches, stockings and buckled shoes and a black gown. Behind him is a low back-rest; behind that, the gold mace. The Woolsack, originally a tribute to the medieval wool trade, is an oblong box covered with red cloth gathered at the corners, and low enough for its occupant to put his feet comfortably on the ground. He raises his hat to the new peer who is by now down on one knee offering him the Letters Patent of his creation. Accepting the scroll on behalf of the Sovereign, he hands it to the Reading Clerk, to be read aloud at the Table to the House. (I must apologise for so many capital letters, but they are correct. Anything handed down from the middle ages tends to run to capitals.)

The Letters Patent take two or three minutes to read. Her Majesty declares,

> that We of Our especial grace, certain knowledge, and mere motion, in pursuance of the Life Peerages Act, 1958, . . . do by these presents advance, create, and prefer, Our trusty and well-beloved . . . to the state, degree, style, dignity, title and honour of . . .

I felt that the medieval language was emphasised by the modern touch in the second line.

Next the Clerk reads aloud at the Table Lord St. John's Writ of Summons by the queen, who commands him to 'be personally present at Our aforesaid parliament . . . to treat and give your counsel upon the affairs aforesaid. . . .' We have already heard the affairs of state described by Her Majesty in the Writ as 'arduous and urgent' and fraught with 'difficulty' and 'dangers'.

His lordship then reads the Oath of Allegiance at the Table and signs the Test Roll. (The present Rolls series dates from 1675, a fresh Roll being started for each parliament and perhaps extending to as much as 120 feet long.) The print of the Oath of Allegiance is so large that I can read its title from way up in the Peeresses' Gallery. Nevertheless new peers, in their relief at having got through the Oath without a stumble, have been known to make off towards the crimson benches without signing the Roll. In which case the Reading Clerk gently nudges them back to the Table. Today, of course, it is possible to use an alternative to the (religious) Oath. Those who have philosophical scruples may instead 'affirm and declare' their loyalty to the Sovereign.

The last scenes in this ancient rite take place on the barons' benches and at the Woolsack. Directed by Garter, all three peers rise up and sit down three times, each time doffing their cocked hats to the Cloth of Estate. Over the years I have noticed considerable differences in this particular performance: most noble threesomes are careful to synchronise their movements, though occasionally there is raggedness; and some threesomes doff their hats with a regular cavalier sweep, while others are content with a stiff brief movement.

Finally, after about ten minutes in all, the Introduction party prepares to leave the Chamber, the new peer stopping on the way out to shake hands with the Lord Chancellor. Those not prepared for it are startled by a sudden subdued roar that ends as abruptly as it began. It is the peers' welcome to the new recruit.

Moments later the observant onlooker may notice a figure, inconspicuously dressed in sober suit and tie, slipping on to one of the back benches. It is the new peer about to begin the business of the day – Questions – timed by a Vulliamy clock in an elegant Gothic case.

If one wants to know more about the history of this impressive ceremony and more about the glowing Chamber in which it takes place, there is an excellent study to turn to. Sir Anthony Wagner, formerly Garter King of Arms, and Sir John Sainty, at present the Clerk of parliament, have combined in their *Origin of the Introduction of Peers* (1967) to surprise us with some unexpected facts. For instance, the present ritual dates from 1621, being the *simpler* version of two much more complex earlier ceremonies. Before 1621 the sovereign himself invested peers of the first creation, personally girding an earl with his sword – hence the term 'belted earl'. The earliest description of a baron's investiture is for the year 1524; 35 years later a Baron St John (no relation) was being invested in the Tower of London. Why the Tower? Not for sinister reasons. The Tower was then one of the royal palaces as well as a prison. After the death of Henry V, succeeding sovereigns preferred more intimate investitures in their own palaces rather than in parliament: Henry VI at his favourite Windsor, Henry VIII at Hampton Court or Greenwich. The old style of ceremony included two supporters, as now, but after it was over the new peer was treated to a glorious dinner at which he sat with the king like a bride at a wedding. Today the meal takes place *before* the Introduction at a luncheon in the Lords' Dining Room for his supporters, family and friends – which he pays for himself.

Garter King of Arms, though, was the greatest beneficiary from the ceremony in the old days. The king gave him largesse and the new peer handed over to him the valuable gown he had been wearing before he donned his parliamentary robe. On the orders of the Earl Marshal in the reign of Elizabeth I, Garter was to have 'the bearing of Letters Patents at the creations of all Noblemen, and their Gowns that they wore before their Creations. . . . And Also the placing of the Lords in parliament and all other assemblies of Honour with all Fees thereunto belonging.' In our own day Garter has to do without the largesse, the fees and even the dark blue or grey suit the new peer is wearing before his Introduction.

Investitures were quietly abandoned during the reign of James I. It was one of those changes that just happened – no documentary evidence – but our authorities, Wagner and Sainty, have made a pretty good guess at the reason why. There were so many creations by James I, and they were all so venal. The king was no doubt glad to be spared the irony of being thanked publicly for an honour which he had *sold* to the recipient. One cannot help wondering what the ghost of James I has made of the sales in our own times!

We can turn to a report by the Victoria and Albert Museum (1974) for an account of the present superb furniture in the House of Lords. The hero of this prodigious achievement was Augustus Welby Pugin, the inventive genius who designed its 280 tables and over 651 seats of various kinds, besides charming standing-desks which the Victorians believed in for health reasons and to save space. Pugin, a Roman Catholic, identified Christian architecture and decoration with the Gothic style. A genial character, he lived for a time by the sea at Ramsgate, generally appearing at his London office in a pilot's uniform. 'There is nothing worth living for,' he used to say, 'but Christian architecture and a boat.'

The 'Christian architecture' for the new buildings of the Houses of parliament – accidentally gutted, as we saw, by fire in 1834 – was provided by another genius, Sir Charles Barry. Within Barry's framework of a Victorian Gothic dream in stone, Pugin embellished his splendid oak furniture with Tudor roses, monograms (VRs predominating), crowns and portcullises (the ancient arms of Westminster), and other symbols of heraldry. They were to focus the minds of peers on the duties that history had handed down to them. The grandest of all the carved oak bookcases, filled with weighty parliamentary volumes, stands in the sombre corridor between the Peers' Library and the Peers' Lobby: a massive construction decorated with linenfold panels, scrolls and leaves.

Some of Pugin's minor furniture has strayed from the various residences within the Palace of Westminster into the rest of the building. 'Pot-cupboards,' reports the V & A, 'turn up in the most unlikely places, performing useful functions quite unlike that originally intended.'

A short book entitled *Works of Art in the House of Lords,* edited by Maurice Bond (H.M.S.O. 1980) tells the story of paintings, sculpture and carvings. Before the fire the medieval Chamber had been hung with 16 enormous tapestries of the Spanish Armada's defeat in 1588. This subject served as a guide to the Fine Arts Commission and its President Prince Albert,.appointed in 1841 to get the House decorated. Their task was to enliven the new Chamber with events from history of which, as before, the nation could be proud. Thus the gauntlet I had noticed on the steps of one fresco was part of *The*

Spirit of Justice (abstract) by Daniel Maclise; the plumed hat in its pair (concrete) belonged to *Prince Henry Acknowledging the Authority of Justice Gascoyne* by C. W. Cope; the harpist appeared in *The Spirit of Chivalry* (Maclise) and its pair was *Edward III conferring the Order of the Garter on the Black Prince* (Cope again). The mitre and the semi-naked king belonged to the last pair of frescoes: *The Spirit of Religion* by J. C. Horsley and *The Baptism of King Ethelbert* by William Dyce. After strenuous modern repair and conservation all six look fine today; they were written off as 'in ruins', though, in 1909, due to climate, outside pollution and the gas jets.

Punch published a skit on Cope's *Prince Henry*, lampooning all the Commission's artists for so earnestly striving to get their historic details absolutely right. Mr Punch himself is shown on the top of a soaring ladder painting a 30-foot fresco (the Chamber's frescoes are 16½ feet high) of Prince Hal *defying* the Lord Chief Justice! 'The costume, I flatter myself, is correct,' boasts Mr Punch. 'The dress was furnished by Tichborne-Street NATHAN. . . .' the famous theatrical costumiers.

The same attention to detail was shown by the artists who painted the Tudor royalties around the Prince's Chamber through which the parliament Chamber is entered at the south end. Though the royal figures were conscientiously copied from contemporary portraits, missals or miniatures, there are some mistakes that would have made *Punch* laugh. Anne Boleyn was taken in error from Anne of Hungary, Katherine Parr from Lady Jane Grey and Jane herself from a Flemish lady. But there is no mistake about Holbein's bursting Henry VIII.

Prince Albert was a brilliant and assiduous chairman of the Commission. He even made a witty joke, remarking to commissioner Lord John Russell when Milton was suggested as a subject for the frescoes: 'You would approve of passages from *Paradise Regained?*' Lord John, a widower, had recently remarried. When Maclise threatened to pack up because his two huge heroic frescoes in the Royal Gallery – *The Death of Nelson* and *The Meeting of Wellington and Blücher at Waterloo* – were fading as he painted them, the devoted Albert rushed up from the Isle of Wight and talked him round.

Pugin's masterpiece is the Throne, based on the Coronation Chair in Westminster Abbey. But unless the Queen or Commissioners representing her is there to open Parliament, this wonderful object is hidden under its red cover; a shade of red which I do not think quite matches up to the crimson carpet of the dais, the red of the low benches on the steps of the Throne (for privy councillors and the eldest sons of peers to sit on) or the gorgeous scarlet leather benches in the Chamber. Perhaps it is the fault of the television lights.

Incidentally, small concealed microphones are slotted into the backs of the peers' benches. The first time I listened to a debate I noticed that several of the older peers were sitting sideways on their benches with their faces resting on the leather, possibly asleep. I did not know about the microphones, until I found one to use myself in the Peeresses' Gallery!

All human institutions can be improved, as we shall see from the pages that follow. Today not even the most jaundiced or satirical critics of the House of Lords could depict it as a gloomy abode of the diseased or deceased. It enjoys brilliance of intellect as well as of television lights and is an active and greatly respected Second Chamber.

INTRODUCTION I

The Palace of Westminster

This is a book about people not buildings. It is the story of a very human institution as it has developed in the last 700 years. But some physical background must be provided. There are at least three admirable books: *Westminster Palace and Parliament* by Patrick Cormack MP, *The Great Palace* by Christopher Jones, and *The Palace of W.* by Sir Robert Cooke, which should be read by all who are interested.

It was the holy Edward the Confessor becoming King in 1042 who built the great Abbey at Westminster. He was buried there, eight years after it had been consecrated, in January 1066. William the Conqueror was anxious to build a new and grander palace for himself. But it was William's son, William Rufus, becoming King in 1087 who took the essential steps to build a truly royal palace. It was indeed from Westminster that the country was governed.

We, however, are concerned with the House of Lords. Edward I (1272–1307) called 16 parliaments in the 35 years of his reign. They sat in the Painted Chamber or in the adjacent White Chamber which in due course became the House of Lords; sometimes in the Chapter House or Refectory in the nearby Abbey. We shall be discussing in the text the series of events that led to the separation of the two Chambers – the House of Lords and House of Commons. By 1377 the separation was complete.

By this time the Lords were established in the White Chamber of the Palace of Westminster, the Commons in the Chapter House of the Abbey. So matters continued until in 1547 the Commons took advantage of a magnificent offer from Edward VI. They moved back across the road to occupy the St Stephen's Chapel within the Palace of Westminster. When the Irish peers joined the Lords after the Union in 1801, the House moved into the former Court of

Requests. In 1834 came the overwhelming disaster of the Great Fire.

Dickens, who witnessed the fire as a young reporter, wrote a memorable account quoted by Patrick Cormack. He begins by explaining that 'a savage mode of keeping accounts by notched sticks' was introduced into the Court of Exchequer. By 1834 this primitive technique had been, in principle, long since abandoned. On the morning of 16 October two workmen began to get rid of two cartloads of the remaining tallies by burning them in a stove which heated the House of Lords . . . an appalling conflagration followed. 'The flames spread rapidly and, though men of the newly established Metropolitan Police soon arrived, and fire engines were quickly on the scene, there was little that could be done to contain the blaze.'

This 'dreadful calamity' as it was called at the time engulfed the Palace of Westminster in devastating fashion. It is not, however, correct to say that all but the great Westminster Hall and the rather insignificant Jewel Tower were reduced to scarred masonry and charred rubble. The famous architect Sir John Soane had rebuilt much of the House of Lords and the Royal Gallery in 1823/24. Much of Soane's work survived the fire, but was (regrettably) demolished to make way for the present building. The Chamber of the Lords was destroyed and Parliament was prorogued on 23 October 1834 – one week after the fire – in the Library of the Lords. After the fire, Parliament met in the Painted Chamber and the Lords' Committee Rooms.

Eventually, after a strenuous competition, Charles, later Sir Charles, Barry, with much assistance from his collaborator Augustus Welby Pugin, constructed what we now know as the Palace of Westminster. The Lords were well satisfied from the beginning and occupied the new chamber in 1847. The Commons, on the other hand, were extremely critical. The new House of Commons was available in 1850 but not finally accepted and made use of until 1853.

Westminster Hall, as already mentioned, remained intact – miraculously it was thought. Certainly a great volume of prayer had gone up for its salvation. It was to survive again in 1941 when the

House of Commons was destroyed by enemy action. When I myself entered the House of Lords in 1945, the House of Commons was still in occupation of our chamber. We performed our functions in the much smaller Robing Room, which would be impossible today with the trebling of our attendance since that time. We returned to our proper place in 1951.

The events with which Westminster Hall is associated are inextricably mixed up with the story of the House either as a political chamber or as the supreme court of the nation. Some of them however do not come under either head – for example, the most famous event of all, the trial of Charles I in 1649. His judges were a small body of commissioners set up by the House of Commons; certainly the House of Lords cannot in any sense be held responsible for his execution. They were themselves on the point of abolition – for the time being. Later I shall be dealing at some length with the trials of the Earl of Strafford and Queen Caroline. Some of the other trials should be mentioned here.

Thomas More's words as he heard his death sentence are justly famous: 'I verily trust and shall therefore heartily pray, though your Lordships have now here in earth been judges to my condemnation, we may yet hereafter in Heaven merrily all meet together, to our everlasting salvation.' He was beheaded on Tower Hill on 6 July 1535, and his head was put on a spike on London Bridge.

Lord Lovat, tried and sentenced to death after the Jacobite rising in 1745, was equally courageous but rather more cynical. As he was led away he turned to his judges: 'Farewell, my Lords. We shall never meet again in the same place, I am sure of that.' In 1760 Earl Ferrers was hanged at Tyburn after being convicted by the peers of murdering his steward. For the well-known trial of Warren Hastings see page 131 below. Guy Fawkes and Titus Oates were both tried in Westminster Hall. The last trial, that of Henry Dundas, first Viscount Melville, charged with using public money for his own ends while Treasurer to the Navy, resulted in the acquittal of Melville who was soon restored to the Privy Council. These trials in Westminster Hall overlap with the story of the House of Lords and can never altogether be banished from our memory when considering events in the political chamber.

INTRODUCTION II

An Afternoon in the House of Lords

14 July 1987, 5.11 pm: Quintin (Lord) Hailsham rises to speak. I am to follow him and concentrate accordingly. This is Quintin Hailsham's first speech since his resignation as Lord Chancellor. He served in that capacity in two governments for twelve years, a record in this century. Quintin was the most brilliant boy of his time at Eton. I was two years senior to him and two years junior to Alec, Lord Home, who is sitting next to him on the 'ex-Ministerial Bench', below the gangway. Alec was the most glamorous figure of my time at Eton, though I don't think that any of us expected him to be Prime Minister. We thought of him as a more likely captain of England at cricket.

One can find everything in the House of Lords today and, sure enough, we have a former cricket captain of England in David Sheppard. It must not be thought that the House of Lords in these latter days is an Old Etonian annexe. Admittedly Quintin Hailsham, Alec Home, Lord Elton, Lord Monson, Viscount Brentford and I myself were Old Etonians in the 21 speakers in this debate but two of the most gifted speakers in the House are the leader of the Labour peers, Lord Cledwyn and Lord Elwyn-Jones, the former Lord Chancellor. Both were brought up Welsh-speaking and educated at Welsh grammar schools. Trade union leaders too have long established themselves. Women are a potent force. At the time of writing there are 67 women in the Lords compared with 40 in the House of Commons. We have no Mrs Thatcher, and are not likely to have a Prime Minister, male or female, but by and large women peers are a much more influential element than women MPs. We have business leaders and professors galore.

At the time of writing there are 1196 members of the House of Lords. Of these nearly 800 are hereditary peers who can pass on their titles to their children. Half of the hereditary peerages have been created in the twentieth century. There are 381 life peers who cannot pass on their titles. There are 26 bishops and 31 law lords.

I should make it clear at once that this is a history of the House of Lords not a history of the aristocracy, a much more nebulous concept. Someone either is or is not a member of the House of Lords, but who shall say whether a particular person is or is not a member of the aristocracy? Almost any general statement on this subject would be disputed. It is a good start to have a title but few would claim that a life peer became an aristocrat by acquiring a life peerage, although he might be judged to be one on other grounds. Most people would agree that the children (and grandchildren? and great grandchildren?) of noble families would be entitled to regard themselves as aristocratic. But how long has a family to be established before it becomes noble – and so on and so forth?

Historically, the aristocracy and the House of Lords have been closely linked. There is some over-lapping today but much less than of old. In his book *Aristocrats* Robert Lacey picks out one English aristocrat, the Duke of Westminster. No one would deny his claims to be an aristocrat, quite apart from the fact that he is possibly the richest man in the country. But he does not come to the House of Lords. If he came he would be valued entirely on his personal merits. Only three out of the 26 non-royal dukes, the Duke of Manchester, the Duke of Norfolk and the Duke of Portland (aged 90), attend regularly, although the Duke of Devonshire has been a minister and is a most attractive speaker.

Peers sometimes inherit their title before they are 21, even in infancy. They join the House when they attain their majority. My brother inherited his earldom at the age of twelve, our father having been killed at Gallipoli. He never took his seat, devoting his life entirely to Ireland. However, when I inherited the title, I found that they had kept a peg for him to hang his coat on in the entrance hall. The average age of the active peers is 66 or thereabouts. The average attendance is somewhere over 300. In the session 1985/6 380 peers attended for at least one-third of the sittings of the House. Of this number, 163 had obtained their titles 'by succession', 217 were created.

The question of the relative strength of the various parties in the House of Lords is more complex than it seems. Taking the official figures of those who accept the Whip or, in the case of the Independents, the equivalent, the figures for December 1986 were as follows:

Conservative	417
Independent (Cross Bench)	245
Labour	118
Liberal	42
Social Democrat	43

Nevertheless a Conservative Government has been defeated on more than 100 occasions in the House of Lords since 1979. In a final chapter I attempt to sum up the realities of the present position.

Quintin Hailsham is a fine oratorical speaker. One passage from his speech gives something of his flavour:

> For some reason, which I think totally inadequate, the attack upon judicial independence normally takes the form of letters by Members of Parliament from all quarters of the other place to the Lord Chancellor of the day. This is a new and, I may say, unwelcome development because it assumes, what is not the case under our constitution, that the Lord Chancellor has some responsibility for disciplining judges who are insufficiently severe in cases of various kinds. . . . Our constitution is based on the independence of the judiciary. That is a rock upon which it has been built ever since 1702, and before 1702 it was a failure to recognise its importance which largely led to the abdication of James II.

When I came to follow Quintin I was happy to welcome him 'coming among us untrammelled'. I reminded the House that it was Gladstone who said: 'I come among you untrammelled.' I continued: 'After admiring the noble and learned Lord for 65 years or more, with every year that passes I think he resembles Mr Gladstone more and more, and I say that by way of a very high compliment.' Quick as a flash my old adversary (I stood unsuccessfully against him at Oxford in 1945) and my much-valued friend put in: 'My Lords, an old man in a hurry', which was what was said of Gladstone at a late point in his career.

These courtesies some people find suffocating, but the longer one remains a member, the more one appreciates them. The politeness of the House of Lords goes back some way. In 1911 passions were running high (see Chapter VIII below), but the language was still one of exaggerated courtesy. I have heard one noble Lord refer to another as 'redolent of oleaginous hypocrisy, without of course any desire to be personally offensive to the noble Lord, for whom I have such a high respect'. Former members of the House of Commons sometimes talk wistfully of the cut and thrust of their previous Chamber, but in my experience they seem to prefer the atmosphere of our own. But we seldom descend to the namby-pamby. Lords Boyd-Carpenter, Orr-Ewing and Beloff on the Conservative side, and Lords Bruce, Molloy and Hatch on the Labour, and Lord Annan amongst others on the cross-benches, make sure that this does not often occur.

No debate is typical. Thirteen out of the 21 speakers in the debate on the Criminal Justice Bill were lawyers. The lawyers incidentally included not only two former Lord Chancellors, Lord Hailsham and Lord Elwyn-Jones, but also Lord Denning (a former Master of the Rolls), two past or present law lords and a former leader of the Criminal Bar, not to mention the eminent solicitor, Lord Mishcon, who advised Jeffrey Archer in his highly successful libel action. Also speaking was a former head of the Home Office. We do not expect the influence of our debates to equal those of the elected Chamber, but on legal matters they carry a special authority. We have much less drama, but distinctly more intellect and far more courtesy.

The peroration of Lord Hailsham gives a little of the flavour of his address: 'I shall sit down after having commented on the impartiality of the judiciary and the independence of the media, Members of Parliament, and, I add with a sly glance at the government bench, of some members of the Cabinet. That independence is at the foundation of our constitution.'

No one who works in the House of Lords for any length of time, either as a peer or as a member of the staff, is unaware of the historical atmosphere or remains unimpressed by it. My wife has given a vivid impression in the Prelude of the scene when new peers are introduced into the House. I am told – and it appears to be true – that as long ago as 1966, when Leader of the House, I suggested that we should be televised. Today, through television, the nation understands much better what it is like to serve in the House of Lords. I am merely one of the innumerable men and women who have drawn much inspiration from the invincible continuity of our House. I have never yet encountered an author who could provide a satisfactory answer to the question: 'Why have you written this book?' But in my case part at least of the answer must be found in my devotion – although never an uncritical devotion – to the House of Lords.

CHAPTER I

1066–1377

The Formation of the House of Lords

When did the House of Lords come into existence? When did it become separate from the House of Commons? Anyone who picks up a book described as a history of the House of Lords will feel entitled to more or less definite answers to these two questions. Three others will rapidly present themselves. When did Parliament begin? When was the representative principle first introduced into British institutions? When did the hereditary principle become the dominant feature of the House of Lords?

Satisfying answers to such questions are not readily available. We must not however be too easily discouraged by the sceptical words of A. F. Pollard in his classic *Evolution of Parliament*, first published in 1920: 'The Lords themselves,' he wrote, 'are still in doubt about their origin; and while they agree on the palpable fiction that Edward I created and intended to create a number of hereditary peerages, they differ as to the date of the creation, and within recent years they have decided that a summons to the parliaments of 1290 and 1293 both did and did not create hereditary peerages.' And much more to the same negative effect.

Nearly 70 years later we must try to be slightly more definite. The history of the House of Lords, however, as of many other institutions, is one of evolution. It is not easy to point dogmatically to the critical dates. Parliament, of which the House of Lords is still described as the Upper House, originated in the councils summoned by English kings in the eleventh, twelfth and thirteenth centuries. But we must go back a little further. The origin of Parliament is sometimes traced to Anglo-Saxon times. In the town-moot the assembled freemen and cultivators of the 'folklands'

27

regulated the civil affairs of their own township, village or parish. Superior to these local institutions was the witenagemot, or 'assembly of wise men', with whom the king took counsel. It is convincingly argued that the witenagemot was the true beginning of the parliament of England. In 1066 the Anglo-Saxon polity was suddenly overthrown. William the Conqueror triumphed at Hastings. He had brought with him the feudal system of France and Normandy. He established it on a firm military basis. Warlike barons and their followers were rewarded with enormous grants of land. The King attached a strict condition of military service in return and a requirement to attend on him when summoned.

Long before the end of the reign of Henry I, the King's Council had almost wholly ceased to be English. The King's advisers were the foreign advisers of a foreign king ruling a subject people. They learned to speak French, intermarried with their rulers, had their children baptised with names imported from France, and at last became indistinguishable from the French themselves. This fusion among the higher ranks was complete towards the end of the reign of Henry II, though it had not affected the lower orders.

In practice the King took council with those whom he thought would be of most assistance to him. Assemblies called in this way were attended by varying numbers of archbishops, bishops and abbots, earls, barons, other lay magnates and royal ministers. I lay stress on the word varied. There was no certainty that someone summoned to attend these Councils would be summoned to attend the next one.

It is easy to lose our way among the various kinds of council known to the law. The Common Council of the Realm, the Great Council, the Secret Council and a Council which did not possess any qualifying epithet. What matters for our purpose is that some of these councils began to be called parliaments. But the word in this context is full of ambiguity.

The *Constitutional History of the House of Lords*, by Luke Owen Pike, published in 1894 but still most valuable, points out that the word parliament 'may be carried back to the reign of The Conqueror'. It appears that an assembly which was held in 1081 is later described in a Law Report of the reign of Edward III as a parliament.

It was not, nor was it represented as being a parliament in the modern sense.

The events which led to the establishment of this assembly (1081) are worth touching on. There was a dispute between the Abbot of Bury St. Edmunds and the Bishop of Thetford about the power of the Bishop to exercise the 'rights of ordinary' over the Abbot. The details do not concern us. It is interesting, however, to note that the persons present in the parliament are described as 'the Archbishop of Canterbury and all the other bishops of the land, earls and barons.' Pike points out that the first assembly in England to which the word parliament has been applied by any legal authority, was an assembly 'resembling the House of Lords in its constitution, but consisting largely of foreigners.'

Professor G. O. Sayles among others has argued that 1258 is the crucial date which marks the conception of organised parliament in England. 'Our knowledge of parliament before 1258 is so fragmented that we find it difficult to differentiate parliament clearly from all other (compulsory) sessions of the King's Council.' He also insists that the servants of the Crown continued throughout the thirteenth century to be much more influential than all those summoned otherwise.

To return to two of our original questions: when did the House of Lords come into existence? When was the representative principle introduced into our constitution? The answer in both cases can only be: somewhere in the thirteenth and fourteenth centuries. It is certainly within the thirteenth century that the crucial steps were taken. It seems to be generally agreed that one cannot find in Magna Carta (1215) the origins of our parliamentary development. An admired writer like Arthur Bryant has said that the pattern of constitutional thought set out in Magna Carta was to be 'reproduced in a thousand forms' in the history of the English and British nation. It was 'a true charter of liberties providing protection on paper at least against the arbitrary rule of the monarchs'. But we must look elsewhere however for the origins of our modern parliaments.

During the thirteenth century, representatives of the communities of the realm from counties, cities and boroughs, were summoned with increasing frequency to assist the king in his deliberations. What was to occur was therefore not utterly novel, but historically it created an all-important precedent. Compared with some other writers Professor Sayles plays down the importance of parliament in the later Middle Ages: 'The salient feature,' he writes, 'of the later Middle Ages was the counsel of the lords wherever it was expressed. The preservation of the balance between the power of the king and the power of the lords was the sum total of mediaeval constitutionalism. Parliament was an expedient of government to be summoned when the king desired a particularly full and representative council. It has been calculated that between 1400 and 1460 forty to fifty "great councils" met and twenty-two parliaments.' Be that as it may, I am not attempting in this book to write a history of the Middle Ages but of the House of Lords. The House of Lords has throughout been a vital part of parliament, and it is on parliament that we must concentrate our gaze.

We must focus on the year 1255. In that year Henry III appealed to the assembled magnates, the country's chief taxpayers with whom he had been quarrelling, to release him and the administration from his almost bottomless debts. The barons' leaders came to the council armed, leaving their swords, however, at the door. They imposed very stringent terms on the King. The King found himself compelled by a body of earls, barons and knights to swear on the Gospels to submit to their advice. The government passed entirely into the hands of a council of 15 which consisted of six earls, six barons and three clerics. All important business was transacted by its authority. The King managed to reassert a measure of control but civil war followed. The King and his son Edward were taken prisoner by Simon de Montfort.

Simon de Montfort, the rebel Earl of Leicester, born in France, has received a generous measure of credit for paving the way (many hundreds of years later) to democracy in Britain. Simon summoned Knights of the Shires and Burgesses from the towns to sit in parliament in 1265. What is so extraordinary is that he summoned his parliament in the King's name while holding the King prisoner. 'Henry, by the grace of God King of England, Lord of Ireland, and Duke of Aquitaine, to the Venerable Father in Christ, Robert by the same grace Bishop of Durham', began the writ sent from Worcester on 14 December 1264. 'Whereas after the great peril of the disorders recently experienced in our kingdom, Edward our dearest first-born son was delivered as a hostage to assure and strengthen the peace of our kingdom, and whereas now that the aforesaid disorders have – thank God! – been quieted, we must treat with our prelates and magnates to make salutary provision for his release, and to establish and consolidate full assurance of peace and tranquillity for the honour of God and the advantage of the whole kingdom . . .'

Simon was soon overthrown and slain, but the process he had set in train was continued. Edward I, coming to the throne in 1272, did not arrive in England until 1274. He held the first parliament of his reign at London on 25 April 1275. Special significance is attached to this parliament by historians today (although the Model Parliament of 1295 held pride of place for many years). It now seems certain that Knights of the Shires were present in 1275 and that burgesses and citizens were also summoned. (The importance of the Model Parliament of 1295 is therefore less than used to be thought.) It should be mentioned that the business of the parliaments included much making and defining of law which was later seen as a series of Statutes. Already a great and apparently increasing mass of petitions was coming before the King and his council in Parliament.

When were the Commons separated from the Lords? There was no doubt that by the end of the fourteenth century they formed a separate House, the House of Commons with its own Speaker and Clerk. The Lords, now in their own House, were usually known either as *domini spirituales et temporales* – 'the Lords Spiritual and Temporal' – or as *domus superior* 'the upper house' – until in the sixteenth century the term 'House of Lords' became normal. It is difficult to be much more precise.

'Various opinions', wrote Luke Owen Pike, 'have been advanced in relation to the time at which the Lords and the Commons began to sit in two separate Houses. Regarded from one point of view the question seems to be almost insoluble; regarded from another it seems extremely simple. It is difficult to prove that a permanent physical barrier was set between the two Houses; it is easy to show that the two Houses were always distinct.'

Ninety years later it is possible to go a little further. The nobles

31

and prelates gathered together to protect their position and little by little they divided into two static groups which sat in two separate houses.

By 1332 the Lords and Commons were meeting in separate chambers. By 1363 the Commons had its own Clerk, a man called Robert de Melton from the Court of Chancery who was paid 100 shillings a year for life, plus any perks he could get; and by 1377 the Commons was so entirely separate from the King and the Lords that it had its own Speaker – that is, the man who spoke to the King on their behalf and had the untrammelled right to do so. 'The Commons' it was certainly called by then, but not yet the 'House of Commons'.

By this time the Commons had adjourned their sittings to the Chapter House of the Abbey of Westminster where they continued to be held after the formal and permanent separation had taken place. For a long time the Commons were far from enthusiastic about their role. They were aware that they were summoned for no other purpose than the taxing of themselves and their fellow townsmen. Their attendance was irksome. It interrupted their own business and their journeys exposed them to many hardships and dangers. Considerable numbers absented themselves from a thankless service. Nevertheless they were increasingly a force to be reckoned with. There came a time when they were no longer content with the humble function of voting subsidies. They boldly insisted on the redress of grievances and further guarantees of national liberties. They remained, however, certainly till 1485 if not later, the inferior House.

The century of the first three Edwards saw the formation of parliament as a political institution, but 'throughout the Middle Ages parliament would develop only within the context of monarchical rule' (G. L. Harriss: *The Formation of Parliament 1272–1377* in *The English Parliament in the Middle Ages*). Edward I was determined that Parliament would be the instrument of the Crown. For 20 years after his return to England in 1274 he summoned Parliament with deliberate regularity at Michaelmas and Easter whenever he was in the realm. On these occasions Edward took counsel on matters at all times, received complaints, provided remedies for abuses by judgement and legislation, and discussed external relations. As time went on Parliament began to wear the aspect of a place of confrontation between King and subjects. For Edward I it became a less attractive forum.

The unhappy reign of Edward II accentuated this trend. The year 1327 marks a plain dividing line. It was then that Parliament, Lords and Commons acting together, showed its teeth. The two Houses refused to supply Edward II with money unless he redressed their grievances. Before the assembled citizens of Westminster and London, they deposed him in a great ceremony in Westminster Hall. As token of his resignation Edward sent his crown and sceptre. Nine months later he was murdered in Berkeley Castle. Even by the standards of those brutal times, the end of Edward II is revolting. Mocked by his jailers as a madman with a crown of plaited straw, he was finished off in a fashion that was supposed to bear some relationship to his homosexual practices. Ultimately he was the victim of his French queen, Isabella, and her exiled lover, Mortimer. His fate was no doubt an indication that no monarch could behave without any reference to the opinions of leading citizens.

Parliament had been summoned for 14 December 1326. The King was in custody by this time and, not unnaturally, refused to attend. This however did not prevent the assembly from deciding on the King's deposition without further delay. Two of the bishops and Henry, Earl of Lancaster, visited the King in prison and persuaded him by a combination of threats and promises to abdicate in favour of his eldest son. Then, 'dressed in black and sobbing', he was led out to the Audience Chamber where he formally resigned his throne. It is worth noting that the delegation to Kenilworth prison provided a 'representation' of the bishops, the earls, the abbots and priors, the barons, the judges, the knights of the shires, the burgesses and the Cinque Ports.

The year 1327 did indeed mark a dividing line in more ways than one. From then on the representatives of the counties and boroughs attended Parliament invariably. Under Edward III, who came to the throne in that year, legislation began to originate from below. In relation to the Commons, the Lords continued throughout the Middle Ages to exercise a certain dominance, which the Commons

33

saw as a traditional protection against tyranny. We must recognise however the overall supremacy of the king, though Edward III weakened somewhat towards the end of his reign.

The origins are obscure of the special petition of the House of Commons in regard to the granting of supply. Even before there was any House of Lords or House of Commons 'payments of money which were independent of the ordinary feudal exactions were perhaps more familiar to the townsmen than to the great feudal lords' (Pike). The burgesses made the best terms they could at the exchequer, but the barons were also ready to assist the King in conjunction with the Commons for a consideration. In 1225, 40 years before that Parliament or assembly which Simon de Montfort caused to be summoned, the archbishops, bishops, abbots, priors, earls, barons, knights, freeholders, and all the King's subjects, gave a fifteenth part of all their moveables in return for a confirmation of the Great Charter and for the Charter of the Forest.

CHAPTER II

1377–1603

The House Settles Down

The period 1377–1422 is of special interest to parliamentary historians. If we were to include the years 1371–1377 also, there were 50 parliaments during the period – almost one a year. But there was no regularity of summons whatsoever. There were three parliaments within ten months in 1382, but none at all between 1373 and 1376, or between 1407 and 1410. The timing was mostly determined by the King's need for a new grant of taxes.

It was not till the reign of Henry IV that a general principle was established. In the second year of his reign (AD 1400), the Commons prayed that before granting supplies they might receive answers to their petitions. The King resisted the plea. A sharp dispute followed. Three points however were finally accepted: supplies were to be granted by the Commons, to have the assent of the Lords and to be reported to the King by the Speaker of the House of Commons. We must remember however that there were long intervals between parliament and parliament. Grants were sometimes made for long periods of time; sometimes for the life of a sovereign. Gradually grants took the form of acts of parliament.

The Lords Spiritual and Temporal (the term came into regular use at the end of the fourteenth century) were summoned individually. When Parliament was in session in the thirteenth and fourteenth centuries, various categories of churchmen were present. The spiritual lords were personally summoned, bishops, abbots or priors. All 21 bishops of England and Wales were as a rule summoned. As for abbots or priors, the full official record for the parliament of 1265 shows that the summons on this occasion of a

35

total of 122 religious superiors was not governed by strict or consistent feudal principles. The number of heads of religious houses summoned, though varying considerably in composition, remained high during Edward I's reign but declined rapidly in Edward II's reign. There is plenty of evidence to show that there was no great desire on their part to attend Parliament.

In addition, royal clerks alongside judges and lay officers were responsible for the administrative and judicial work of parliament; and a number of royal officials, lay and clerical, including masters, or principal clerks of chancery, were summoned personally to be present with the king and 'with the others of our council.' The summons of the Lords Temporal is a more complicated subject. Dukes, marquesses, earls and barons were normally summoned to Parliament if they were of age, but summons was not a matter of legal right. The three highest ranks formed what was almost a group apart. 'Earl' was an ancient title. The first English duke (Edward of Woodstock) had been created only in 1337 and the first marquess by Richard II, Robert de Vere, Earl of Oxford, who was created Marquis of Dublin [sic] in 1385. The summoning of barons was haphazard in the early days, but gradually repeated summons led to uniformity and 'to the evolution of a definable group of barons whose titles by the mid-fifteenth century were to be matters of hereditary status, not tenure.' (A. L. Brown: *Parliament 1377–1422* in *The English Parliament in the Middle Ages*).

The Lords were nominally a body of about 100. Up to 1400 the lay lords were normally in a slight majority, but thereafter the opposite was true. It is reckoned that often less than half of those summoned actually attended. (We know all about that in these latter days too.) The Lords in session usually consisted of about 40 peers. They included the great officers, even if they were not peers, and up to 13 judges and lawyers when their professional advice was required. These 40 peers were much the same men who were summoned to great councils, assemblies especially summoned by writ under the Privy Seal, meeting more often than parliaments, discussing matters of state, but no longer with power to tax or enact statutes. The lords who attended Parliament were men of much experience and power and were frequently involved in bitter disputes among themselves. The Commons were a body of more than 250 (nominal) members.

1399 was another of the traumatic years. Richard II, who had started so heroically, had hopelessly over-reached himself and, reputedly, had at the same time lost the appetite for rule. By May of 1399 he was the prisoner of the future Henry IV. On the day before Parliament met, 'certain lords spiritual and temporal, judges and others skilled in civil, canon and common law, being assembled in the accustomed place of his council at Westminster', sent a deputation to wait upon King Richard in the Tower. To this deputation the King delivered a comprehensive Deed of Abdication, under what pressure no one will ever know. It is worth noticing that the Knights of the Shires and the Burgesses were not represented. Instead the bishops, earls and barons were accompanied by a strong representation of the law. The Archbishop of York now proceeded to declare the fact of the Abdication to a great assembly in Westminster Hall.

It was put to the Lords Spiritual and Temporal, one by one, then to the Commons and then to all those assembled including the bystanders. This, however, was not considered quite sufficient. All three estates, Lords Spiritual, Lords Temporal and the Commons jointly and separately agreed to inform Richard of the deposition and to withdraw their fealties. It was not, of course, the first time that the realm had deposed a King. A similar deposition had been carried out into effect (see above) by an assembly summoned as Parliament by the King himself. The Assembly which purported to have accepted Richard's abdication and for greater insurance to depose him never called itself a Parliament. As Enoch Powell points out in his learned history of the House of Lords up to 1540, the whole conception of the Three Estates was full of ambiguities and indeed absurdities.

We all remember the sentiments attributed to Richard by Shakespeare:

> 'I give this heavy weight from off my head,
> And this unwieldy sceptre from my hand,
> The pride of kingly sway from out my heart,
> With mine own tears I wash away my balm,

With mine own hands I give away my crown,
With mine own tongue deny my sacred state.'

What he really felt is too painful to dwell on.

During the fifteenth century the consent of the Commons to the passing of Acts of Parliament became essential, but the Lords on their side obtained some increase of privileges and status. In this period they came to be referred to as the Higher or Upper House; the Commons as the Lower or the Commons. Bishop Stubbs had treated developments in the fifteenth century as trivial, but A. R. Myers will have none of that. He admits, however, that Henry VII held only one parliament lasting nine weeks during the last twelve years of his reign. Henry managed to get by without many parliaments because of his careful housekeeping and formidable efficiency in collecting taxes. By the end of the fifteenth century Parliament was still an occasional assembly. In a sense it remained one until the 'Glorious Revolution' of 1688.

The older nobles were often said to have destroyed themselves in the Wars of the Roses. This is now considered to be incorrect. Nevertheless only 29 temporal peers were summoned to the first parliament of Henry VII in 1485. Richard III, having as we must presume, on balance of evidence, murdered the Princes in the Tower, had become the last monarch to be slain in battle. However, compensations for the aristocracy were on the way.

When did the inheritance of a peerage acquire the automatic right to membership of the House of Lords? The transition was very gradual. English peers began to speak of themselves as peers of the realm in the reign of Edward II, which shows an increased sense of their dignity. Along with the development of their hereditary rights, however, went the assertion of the monarch of his right to summon a man if he wished. Richard II tried to do this when he summoned John Beauchamp, the steward of his household to Parliament in 1387, after creating him by Letters Patent Lord Beauchamp and Baron of Kidderminster. Beauchamp was 'appealed' in Parliament by the King's foes and beheaded. In 1441, however, Henry VI who had been declared of age in 1437 issued a Patent which announced that:

By the advice of our council we have created our beloved and trusty knight, Ralph Boteler, our chamberlain, to be Baron of Sudeley in the County of Gloucester . . . and have invested, adorned, and ennobled him with the pre-eminences, dignities . . . pertaining to . . . the status of a baron of our realm of England, both in sitting in our parliaments and councils and everywhere else, and wish him to be called a noble of our realm; to have and to hold the name . . . to himself and the heirs male of his body lawfully begotten in perpetuity.

This is regarded as an important landmark in the history of the lords of parliament. From this time there were two kinds of lords of parliament. The increasing number like Lord Sudeley were peers created by Letters Patent in tail male, the title passing to men only. The remainder who were all the time being diminished by extinction were peers by prescription as heirs of estates whose holders had been summoned by writ in the fourteenth or thirteenth century.

In one way or another the summons to Parliament became hereditary and no longer depended on the caprice of the sovereign. It seems impossible to put one's finger on the moment when this major change occurred.

The House of Lords in The Tudor Period

The history of Parliament in the period 1485–1603 is a battleground of historians. The orthodoxy for many years formulated by A. F. Pollard and brought to completion by J. E. Neale is that Parliament 'rose' in legislative and political authority under the Tudors.

The orthodox school which held sway for so long treated the Commons as having superseded the Lords as the more important legislative chamber. 'Thereafter,' as the doctrine has been summarised by Michael Graves, 'the House of Lords slithered from its superiority towards political impotence.' Graves goes on to complain: 'repeatedly we are told that there is little to be learned about the Elizabethan lords'. In the late 1960s and 1970s there emerged a revisionist attitude. As a result the Commons has been displaced from its central role in Tudor parliamentary history.

There has been a notable rehabilitation of the Lords. To some extent the two Houses rose and fell together. When the king or queen did not choose to summon parliament, that applied to Lords and Commons alike. Henry VII began by calling parliaments every two years while he was establishing himself. Only three however met in the last 18 years, averaging eight or nine weeks apiece. No one seemed to complain. Henry VIII began by calling six parliaments between 1510 and 1515 but his chief minister, Cardinal Wolsey, found them awkward customers; only one more parliament was summoned before Wolsey's fall in 1529. Henry, however, needed Parliament and made very skilful use of it while carrying through the crucial policies of the Reformation. Between 1529 and 1532 Parliament dutifully assisted Henry in his unsuccessful attempts to coerce Pope Clement VII who alone could annul his marriage to Catherine of Aragon. Then it did all he asked in the crisis that followed. An Act of Parliament established his competence to deal in matters of spiritual law and enabled Henry to secure the annulment, marry Anne Boleyn, and guarantee the legitimacy of their offspring. In 1533/34 Parliament proceeded to enact the statutory rejection of papal supremacy and the declaration of a national Catholic church with the King as its supreme head.

England and Wales were united by statute. By statute, in 1536, the monasteries were dissolved and their property transferred to the Crown. For Enoch Powell and other writers, the most revolutionary change in the whole history of the House of Lords was the removal of the abbots from the Chamber as a result of the Dissolution. Pike takes a similar view. He has no doubt at all that 'the most important of all permanent changes ever effected at any one time in the constituent parts of the House of Lords was that which befell when the greater monasteries were dissolved'.

Up to that time the spiritual lords had been commonly equal, if not superior in numbers to the temporal lords. But the power of the Crown had greatly increased since the Wars of the Roses. Most of

the abbots and priors made a voluntary surrender of their possessions. An abbot who attempted to retain his abbey and his spiritual
dignity would usually have paid the penalty with his life. The effect
of the Dissolution of the Monasteries was irreversible. The abbots
and priors ceased to sit in Parliament and the King had their lands at
his disposal. The Lords Spiritual reduced to bishops and archbishops could never again command a majority in the House of
Lords.

The few new bishoprics created by Henry left the Lords Spiritual
in such a minority that the Lords Temporal outnumbered them in
the proportion of about two to one. Today there are still 26 bishops
in a House of nominally more than 1000 members.

With the assistance of Michael Graves, we will take a look at the
House of Lords during the reign of Edward VI and Mary I. The
peerage comprised a small social élite which after an initial increase
remained stable in numbers throughout the sixteenth century: 43 in
1509, 54 in 1529 and 53 in 1563. Attrition was sometimes the simple
consequence of natural causes through lack of heirs. State action
also took its toll, usually through the process of attainder for treason
whereby a dignity became forfeit. Three peers suffered the full
penalty for treason. Lord Seymour of Sudeley was executed in 1549
for 'High Treason, great falsehodes, and marvelous heynous misdemeanours against the Kinges Majestes person and his Royall
Crowne'. The Duke of Northumberland died for his attempt to alter
the succession in favour of Lady Jane Grey in 1553. And another
duke, Suffolk, suffered less than a year later for his pathetic and
abortive attempt to raise the Midlands against Mary and her
proposed Spanish marriage. In December 1551 the fourth duke of
Somerset successfully defended himself against a charge of treason
but was condemned and executed for felony. He was posthumously
attainted by statute, whereby all honours were forfeit.

But new creations and restorations kept the score level. Surrey
was accused of planning to endanger the succession of Prince
Edward to the throne of King Henry VIII who was understood to be
dying. Surrey was credited with the intention of diverting the Crown
into the hands of his own family. We are told that no testimony of
serious legal value was produced against him. He firmly denied that

41

he had any treasonable intention, but he was proved guilty and beheaded on Tower Hill. For his father's rehabilitation see below (page 46).

The size of the episcopacy was decided by the number of existing dioceses. It also depended on the Crown's rapidity in filling vacancies. The Edwardian and Marian episcopacy experienced nearly 50 changes. Eighteen deaths and nine promotions were the consequences of the inexorable march of time. But the rest were the result of the successive changes of religion.

There were various reasons for temporary disqualification of a peer. It was not in fact until May 1685 that the Lords formally resolved 'that no lord under the age of one and twenty years should be permitted to sit in the House'. Long before that, however, some such rule was in force. Poverty was another disability. Henry Grey who succeeded his brother as fourth Earl of Kent in 1523 surrendered the earldom 'by reason of his slender estate'. Thereafter he styled himself Sir Henry Grey.

It is clear that the Crown exercised some discretionary powers in cases of minority, poverty and lunacy. Sometimes peers had been placed under restraint whether by close imprisonment, house arrest or enforced exile in the country. It will be seen from these references that the monarch of the day possessed considerable freedom in deciding who could or could not take their seats. On the whole it seems that the monarch pursued an uncontroversial course. 'There were no dramatic sessional fluctuations which might point to unusual manipulative activity by the Crown'. (Graves). The total nominal membership, that is counting the spiritual lords, fluctuated round the figure of 80. Graves estimates the actual membership as fluctuating between 65 and 79. We should bear in mind that during the mid-Tudor period the Commons expanded from 343 to 400 members.

The business of the House was primarily legislation. We can make a rough estimate of the productivity of Parliament by the enactment of statutes. Between the accession of Edward VI and the death of Mary (1547–1558) 747 Bills were submitted to Parliament or devised by it. Only 35% began their parliamentary passage in the House of Lords and some of them were too minor to be significant.

When it comes, however, to Bills actually passed into law, the Lords had a much higher success rate. Well over half the Acts began there. It can fairly be claimed that the Lords during this period were scarcely inferior to the Commons in the importance of the legislation which they initiated.

The Lords seems to have been considerably the more efficient of the two. It had a higher proportion of experienced members and the legal assistants were at its beck and call. But there seems to have been a dramatic deterioration in the Parliament under Mary; briefer sessions, fewer statutes, inferior standards of recording and declining attendance. There followed a shrinkage in its business and a decline in its initiating role. We are presented with a very sharp contrast between the reigns of Edward VI and Mary in these respects.

During the reign of Edward both Houses were active and co-operative, with the Lords exercising the more formative influence of the two. But with Mary, after a happy beginning, relations grew sour between the House of Lords and the Queen. In Mary's fourth parliament the Lords surrendered the critical influence to the Commons and never recovered it. We are left to conclude that Mary's controversial religious policies led in one way or another to a weakening of the Lords' position. It seems beyond question that the reputation and reliability of the Lords sagged during the earlier Marian parliaments.

We must confine ourselves to a few outstanding features of the Elizabethan House. The number of bishoprics remained constant at 26 throughout the reign, while the peerage fluctuated between a nominal 65 and 52. Such, however, was the effect of wastage and the six attainders for treason that by the end of the reign a third of the total owed their noble rank to the Queen. Michael Graves refers to them as exclusive, select and above all few in number – the members of a small chamber which was diminishing in size.

The number and proportion of Bills which commenced in the Lords declined. Nevertheless the Lords remained prominent in the legislative process during the reign of Elizabeth I (1558–1603), partly as the result of the presence there from 1571 to 1598 of Elizabeth's chief minister, Lord Burghley. The Lords seem to have been more efficient. In the years 1572 to 1581, 42% of its Bills became law, but only 18% of those promoted by the Commons did so. The Lords were the institutional equal of the Commons and in its social and political influence much superior. At times there were sensitive little disputes. Charles, Lord Stourton (ancestor of the present) had been executed for murder in the previous reign. This, though it did not extinguish the title, tainted the blood of the culprit's descendants. When the heir, John, Lord Stourton, attained his majority, Elizabeth signed a Grace Bill which would restore him in blood and so enable him to inherit property and defend his rights in the Law Courts. The Grace Bill passed the Lords smoothly but the Commons modified it, incensed by the Lords' rejection of a Bill which they had passed a few days before. A tremendous row followed. The Bill failed to pass.

Taking the reign as a whole it cannot be denied that the Commons became the chief initiator of Bills and progressively increased its share of business. But the peers' political influence as a social élite 'strengthened the collective authority of the House' (so writes Michael Graves). One turns for a final comment to *The Parliament of England 1559–1581* by Professor Elton. It is bleak enough: 'In politics, parliament was only a secondary instrument to be used or ignored by agencies whose real power base and arena of activity lay elsewhere – at Court or in Council. And even, as in taxation and legislation the House of Commons took a greater share of the action than the House of Lords, so in matters of politics it was even weaker and more irrelevant than the peers upstairs.' He rounds off the passage still more sharply. 'All talk of the rise of parliament as an institution or worse the rise of the House of Commons into political prominence is balderdash.' I do not presume to quarrel with Professor Elton's verdict.

INTERLUDE I

Some Noble Families

Many noble families have been prominent in the history of the House of Lords. I would like to select a few of them to represent them all. Howard, Stanley, Russell, Cecil, Mowbray and Stourton, de Ros. No writer of fiction could improve on the dramatic fortunes of these noble lines.

The House of Norfolk

Take, for example, the first four Dukes of Norfolk of the Howard family. The whole story of the family has been wonderfully well told by John Martin Robinson. Sir Robert Howard, who died in 1436, made a most brilliant marriage in 1420 which has been described by Robinson as the foundation of all the subsequent glories of the Howard line. His bride was Lady Margaret Mowbray, elder daughter of Thomas Mowbray, Duke of Norfolk and Earl Marshal of England. This last position since 1672 adheres to the Dukes of Norfolk.

John Howard, the son of Sir Robert, went on from strength to strength. On 28 June 1483, barely a week after Richard III's accession to the throne, Howard was created Duke of Norfolk, Marshal and Earl Marshal of England, and granted his share of the Mowbray estates. At the coronation of Richard III on 6 July, Norfolk officiated as Lord High Steward as well as Earl Marshal. On 25 July he was created Lord Admiral of England, Ireland and Aquitaine, Surveyor of Array in Norfolk, Suffolk and eleven other counties,

Steward of the Duchy of Lancaster and a member of the Privy Council.

Still faithful to Richard, indeed leading the van, he was slaughtered at the Battle of Bosworth in 1485. Two months later he was posthumously attainted; his son was attainted along with him. But the second Duke showed remarkable powers of recovery – he became one of Henry VII's leading ministers and in due course regained possession of his lands. He died in 1524, aged 80. He was given a funeral which was, in Robinson's words, 'the last of its kind. . . . No nobleman was ever to be buried in such style again.' His will was the last in which a subject spoke of himself as 'we'. Not a bad finale for someone who began his career under attainder!

His ups and downs were if anything surpassed by those of the third Duke. The latter was for a long period the most powerful nobleman in England. He was the uncle of two queens of England, both of whom were executed.

In the latter case, that of Katherine Howard, he saved himself by denouncing his niece's behaviour with tears in his eyes. He laughed when sentence was passed against her. Not in fact a savoury character, as is well known to all students of Shakespeare. He was chiefly responsible for the overthrow of both Wolsey and Thomas Cromwell. He arrested the latter personally at the Council table. 'My Lord: I arrest you of high treason', he shouted, as he tore the George from the minister's neck and trampled it under his heel: 'You shall be judged by the bloody laws you yourself have made.' Cromwell was beheaded under an Act of Attainder.

But Norfolk's own life was soon placed in peril, as a result of the rise to supreme power of the Seymours. His son was arrested; he himself was put in the Tower. Nothing could have saved him except the death of the King which occurred on the very morning of the day on which he was to be beheaded. He spent the whole of the reign of Edward VI imprisoned in the Tower, but on the accession of Mary there was a total reversal of his fortunes: the attainder was reversed and his title and estates restored to him. He was reinstalled as a Knight of the Garter and member of the Privy Council. He died in 1554, aged 80 (like his father) and, again like his father, the greatest nobleman in the country. They had both survived and triumphed.

The fourth Duke underwent the opposite change of fortune. He was attainted and executed for attempting to marry Mary Queen of Scots and supposedly being involved in an international Catholic plot. This allegedly would have involved the Pope and Philip II of Spain in the overthrow of Elizabeth, her replacement with Mary Queen of Scots and the restoration of the Catholic religion in England. There seems no doubt about his sincere Protestantism. But clearly his admitted desire to marry Mary Queen of Scots was the kind of error which the Dukes of Norfolk, by and large, have avoided. There it is. The first four Dukes were attainted, but two of them, the second and the third, recovered gloriously. The first was slain in battle. Only the fourth was executed. But the Earl of Surrey, 'the poet Earl', son of the third Duke, was also beheaded. The eldest son of the fourth Duke is now known as 'Saint Philip Howard', having been canonised in 1970. He died in 1595, aged 38, having lost his titles, his estates, his houses, all his worldly possessions and having been forcibly separated from his wife for over ten years.

Taking the first four Dukes of Norfolk and two of their eldest sons who ended their lives between 1485 and 1595, one cannot imagine greater extremes of grandeur and misery.

The House of Stanley

A family due to become all-powerful in the north-west part of England, the Stanleys enjoyed during the last years of the fifteenth and throughout the sixteenth century more consistent fortune than the Howards, though it was marred by tragedy. By 1385 Sir John Stanley found himself a very rich and influential landholder in south-west Lancashire. His marriage to Isabel Laythom was the foundation of the family soon to be known as the Stanleys of Laythom and Knowsley. John Stanley benefitted much from the goodwill of Richard II. But when in 1399 Henry of Lancaster (later Henry IV) landed at the mouth of the Humber, John Stanley 'stole away' (to use the expression of Bageley, authorised biographer of the Earls of Derby) to join Henry's cause. What followed is put succinctly by Bageley: 'Service under King Henry IV enriched him even more. He received another half-dozen estates in Cheshire and was soon granted the Lordship of Man.'

Throughout the fifteenth century the Stanleys pursued their own interests astutely. Henry VI made Sir Thomas Stanley, Baron Stanley in 1466 and admitted him to the Order of the Garter. During the Wars of the Roses the Stanley of the day moved adroitly from side to side. When Edward IV came out on top, Stanley was sufficiently important for Edward to ignore his recent support for Henry VI. Stanley resumed his seat in the council and gratefully accepted the post of Lord Steward of the Household. When Richard III seized power, Stanley appeared to be one of his principal allies. But when the crunch came at Market Bosworth in 1485, Stanley halted his troops at Stoke Golding where he was strategically placed to help either side, and distant enough to avoid being involved in the first stages of the battle. When the battle was over, Stanley claimed that his last-minute intervention on the side of Henry VII had turned the tide of battle. Neither Richard II nor Richard III had much for which to thank the Stanleys.

Stanley, not surprisingly, was soon created Earl of Derby by the grateful Henry. (It should be mentioned that Henry's widowed mother became Stanley's second wife, so that Stanley was the new King's step-father.) Catastrophe now intervened to mar the happy scene. The new earl's younger brother William became involved in the plot to bring Perkin Warbeck to the throne. He was duly executed. Stanley must have been a fairly cold-blooded type. We are told by Bageley: 'Outwardly at least he shewed no resentment, even when William was executed.'

From now on the Earls of Derby must be thought of as occupying a semi-royal status in Lancashire and adjacent areas. We need not trace the expansion of their property in detail. It must be said in their favour that they maintained a more tolerant attitude towards Roman Catholics, of whom there were many in their area, than other Protestant leaders. When Mary I came to the throne (1553), Earl Edward, recently appointed Lord High Steward, carried the Sword of State before her. To demonstrate his own wealth and importance Edward took with him 80 gentlemen 'in coats of velvet' and more than twice as many liveried retainers. All displayed the eagle emblem of the Stanleys.

When Queen Mary died and Elizabeth came to the throne (1558) Stanley lost little time in returning to London to pay his respects to the new Queen. On the whole, the Stanleys fared well whoever was on the throne until the Civil War.

The House of Russell

Having dissolved the monasteries, Henry VIII handed out to peers or courtiers who soon entered the peerage much of the expropriated wealth. In the long run few families benefited more than the House of Russell. They can plausibly claim to be the most distinguished family in English history. Their only strong rivals would be the Cecils (see below). In the last 100 years the Barings with six peerages, the Trevelyans and Huxleys, with outstanding services to the country and to culture, cannot be overlooked. But over the last 500 years the Russells, with the possible exception of the Cecils, must occupy the first place.

A learned if partly fictional history of the family was published in 1833 by J. H. Wiffen, describing himself as a corresponding member of the Society of Antiquaries of Normandy. Wiffen starts the family tree with Olaf, the sharp-eyed King of Rerik, and proceeds to include various kings 'of the Danes' and Sweden. More prosaic historians view such claims with scepticism. One writes: 'Obsequious genealogists have traced their lineage from Hugh de Rozel, alias "Hugh Bertrand, Lord of le Rozel", a companion of the Conqueror, padding their fiction with the pedigree of certain Russells who are found holding Kingston Russell in Dorset as early as the reign of King John. But the first undoubted ancestor of the Bedford line is Stephen Gascoigne (*alias* Russell) of Weymouth and Bordeaux, wine merchant. Then came Henry Russell, a Weymouth merchant, returned as burgess for that borough in four parliaments between 1425 and 1442.'

It is probable that the ducal house of Bedford springs from a family of Gascon wine merchants settled in a part of Dorsetshire where many Frenchmen settled. For our purposes, the story really begins with John Russell who was born in 1486 and died in 1555. He had already begun to make his mark under Henry VII, but it was under Henry VIII that he rapidly emerged as a soldier and diplomatic agent, marrying a rich widow en route. He became Lord Russell of Chenies in Buckinghamshire (where his wife had brought him much property) in 1539, and acquired the Garter in the same year. Having held many high offices he was named by Henry VIII as one of his executors. His progress continued naturally enough during the short reign of Edward VI. He was raised to the earldom of Bedford in 1550. What is much more surprising is that he continued to prosper under Queen Mary. Not only was he a floating worshipper, but he had played an active part in trying to install Lady Jane Grey as queen. Wiffen writes blandly enough: 'Mary certainly behaved with a wise moderation.' The Earl of Bedford was reinstated as Lord Privy Seal. When he died in London in 1555 he left a vast estate of ex-church lands.

The fifth Earl of Bedford pursued the usual course during the Civil War. He fought first for Parliament and then for the King. After that he concentrated on domestic matters completing, for example, the drainage of the 'Bedford Level'. 'During the Commonwealth and Protectorate,' wrote Wiffen, 'the Earl of Bedford found an agreeable relief from the distractions of the time in the bosom of his family which consisted of seven sons and three daughters.'

None of this seems to have counted against him either with the Cromwellians or Charles II at the Restoration in 1660. Bedford carried St Edward's staff at the crowning and seems to have remained in good standing thereafter. The great tragedy of his life was the execution of his son, Lord Russell, in 1683, who was accused of conspiring to assassinate the King. When finally William of Orange arrived in England in 1688 to be crowned King as William III of England, he 'amply redeemed' (to quote Wiffen) 'promises which he had made to the Russell family when Prince of Orange'. One of the first acts of his government was to reverse the attainder of Lord Russell and a vote of the House of Commons stigmatised his execution as murder.

The venerable Earl of Bedford was in 1694 created a Duke. A similar honour was conferred on the Earl of Devonshire, a bosom friend of his executed son. The Duke would probably wish to be remembered by his reply to King James II somewhat earlier, when the latter came to him for support. 'My Lord,' he said to Bedford, 'you are a good man; you have interest with the peers and can render me today essential service.' Bedford replied, 'For myself, Sir, I am old and weak; but I had once a *son* who could indeed have served your Majesty.' But James could be forgiven for not looking upon Lord William Russell in quite that light.

An illustration of the stature of the Bedfords can be found at the end of the eighteenth century, when the Duke of Bedford of the day was rash enough to support Lord Lauderdale in attacking the grant of a pension to Edmund Burke on his retirement from Parliament. Burke immortalised the Duke in question in his famous *Letter to a Noble Lord*. Had not the Duke's ancestor received grants from Henry VIII that were 'so enormous, as not only to outrage the economy, but even to stagger credibility? The Duke of Bedford is the Leviathan among all creatures of the Crown. He tumbles about his unwieldy bulk; he plays and frolics in the ocean of the Royal bounty. Huge as he is, and whilst "he is floating many a rood" he is still a creature. His ribs, his fins, his whalebone, his blubber, the very spiracle through which he spouts a torrent of brine against his origin, and covers me all over with spray, – every thing of him and about him is from the Throne. Is it for *him* to question the Royal favour?'

Georgiana Blakiston, the gifted author of *Woburn and the Russells*, insists that 'there is no evidence that Lord Bedford was a more shameless beggar than others; ten peers received larger grants than he did'. Be that as it may, he came out remarkably well. He received the reversion of the Abbey lands of Woburn; he received grants of land in Devonshire and Cornwall, in Northamptonshire and Buckinghamshire and Bedfordshire, and a large part of the domain that had belonged to Thorney Abbey in Cambridgeshire. Covent Garden and the seven acres of Long Acre – part of the estates of the Duke of Somerset – were granted to him after the attainder of that nobleman. It may be that the source of so much of their wealth promoted their antipathy of the Catholic Church, which was to be displayed not infrequently by members of the Russell family.

The first Earl's son, Francis (1527–1585) appears to have inherited his father's adroitness. He had been involved in what is known as Wyatt's plot and escaped to the Continent, joining the Protestant exiles in Geneva. He returned however in 1557 and, like his father, was employed by Queen Mary, who died soon afterwards. Her alleged bigotry seems to have been moderated in the case of the Russells. Francis prospered, as we might expect, under Queen Elizabeth, emerging without obvious discredit from the execution of his friend the Duke of Norfolk (see above).

Bedford pleaded with the Queen through Sir William Cecil for Norfolk's life. 'The Duke's liberty I should like well of, praying God it may be in all things such as it should be for God's glory and the Queen's honour.' The moment came however when he was convinced that Norfolk was incorrigible. Bedford was among the peers who sat upon Norfolk's trial and who adjudged him guilty.

The third earl need not detain us, but the fourth earl who succeeded in 1627 comes down to us as one of the great might-have-beens of history. (See below, page 69).

The House of Cecil

When I became a member of the House of Lords in 1945, it was impossible not to feel the all-pervading presence of the Cecils. The fifth marquis, 'Bobbity' was still active and much admired in the House. He had been Leader of the House or of the Opposition in the Lords from 1942 to 1957, and had been throughout that time the leading personality there. His father's bust was in the corridor just opposite the entry to the dining room; his grandfather's portrait was in the same corridor, shown destroying the Home Rule Bill of 1893. His great-grandfather's photograph was in the room I later occupied as Leader. Four generations of Salisburys, successive Leaders of the House of Lords. An awe-inspiring record.

Bobbity Salisbury I leave over till the post-war section of this book. In studying the rest of the family, one is much indebted to two brilliant volumes: *The Cecils of Hatfield House* (1973) by Lord David Cecil and *The Later Cecils* (1975) by Kenneth Rose. Lloyd George on one occasion assured Lord Robert Cecil that 'he was a Welshman'. A soldier from the Welsh border, he (Robert) is said to have fought with Henry VII at the Battle of Bosworth. His grandson, William (1520–1598) became by far the closest and most influential of Queen Elizabeth's counsellors. He was created Lord Burghley by her. Lord David Cecil describes Queen Elizabeth as 'the most famous of English monarchs'. He has no hesitation in announcing that 'she deserves her fame'. That opinion, while not beyond dispute, is widely shared. William Cecil helped her more than any other man.

During the reign of Henry VIII he had begun to make his way forward, incidentally being placed in charge of the business affairs of Princess Elizabeth. His progress continued under Edward VI. Somewhat reluctantly he was ready to support the claim of Lady Jane Grey, but when Mary came to the throne he made his peace with her without much difficulty. Like Elizabeth, William Cecil felt no difficulty in attending Mass as a sign of outward conformity, but he prudently retired to the country. 'As a relaxation,' says Lord David, 'he started building two great Houses for himself, one at Burghley near Stamford, and one in London.' He was at all times much concerned to promote the interests of the State, but also those of his own family. By the time his son Robert (1563–1612) was thirty, William was in a position to appoint him as his deputy. Robert was small, his back was rounded, but in his own way he was just as potent as his father. By discreet moves before the death of Elizabeth he effected the peaceful emergence of James VI of Scotland as James I of England in 1603.

From that day to this, the Cecils have enjoyed a reputation for a certain ruthlessness when their minds are thoroughly made up. Two examples can be provided from these early years. There came a moment when William Cecil strongly favoured the execution of Mary Queen of Scots as absolutely necessary, both for the safety of England and of Elizabeth's own life. Elizabeth finally gave in. After Mary's execution William was banished from her presence for four whole months – to cover up, it might seem, her own guilt.

Robert, in his turn, was just as determined that the Earl of Essex should pay the penalty for his disloyalty: 'As you have showed yourself a rebellious traitor,' he told the charismatic earl, 'you shall die an impudent traitor.' In spite of their worldly successes, both Cecils suffered in their last years (Robert was only 49 when he died) from a sense of failure. But each made an edifying death. Lying in his bed, William could be heard in his prayers 'Lord have mercy. . . . Come Lord Jesus, one drop of death, Lord Jesus.' Robert, who it should be mentioned became the first Lord Salisbury, experienced a kind of ecstasy towards the end. 'O Lord Jesus,' he cried, 'sweet Jesus, now let me come unto thee . . . Thy will be done, I am saved, I am saved.' He lingered on, but not for much longer. 'I desire,' he had said, 'to go without noise or vanity out of this vale of misery, as a man who had long been satiated with terrestrial glory.'

Lord Mowbray and Stourton

In Burke's Peerage we come across this entry: 'The 26th Baron Mowbray, 27th Baron Segrave and 23rd Baron Stourton. His Lordship is heir general of the houses of Howard and Talbot (of which his heirs male are the Duke of Norfolk and Earl of Shrewsbury) and is senior co-heir to the earldom of Norfolk (1312) and to the baronies of Talbot, Howard, Strange de Blackmere, Braose of Gower, Greystock, Dacre of Gillesland, Ferrers of Wemme, Verdon, Darcy of Darcy, Giffard of Brimmesfield, and co-heir to the baronies of Kerdeston, Dagworth, Fitz-Warine, Fitz-Payne, Argentine, Darcy of Darcy, etc. He claims as Lord Mowbray to be Premier Baron of England.'

For what my opinion is worth, I am sure that my friend Charles Mowbray, as we call him, is justified in the claim. It is worth studying the note which Burke attaches to this entry: 'The House of Lords on 26 July 1877 resolved that it was proved by the Writ of Summons addressed to Roger de Mowbray in 11 Edward I (1283) and the other evidence that the Barony of Mowbray was in the reign of Edward I vested in Roger de Mowbray. It was therefore regarded as proved that Roger Lord Mowbray was summoned to parliament "by one of the earliest Writs which could create a peerage".' By similar reasoning Lord Stourton was able to establish his claims to the titles of Mowbray and Segrave.

An ancient peerage certainly. But the claim to the senior barony has been more controversial. The ancestor of Lord Mowbray was summoned in 1283, the ancestor of the Lord de Ros in 1264. But when these matters were brought before the House of Lords in 1877, it was pointed out that Robert de Ros, first Baron de Ros, took an active part against the King. He was one of the Chief Barons who, after the Battle of Lewes in 1264, where Henry III and his son, Prince Edward, became prisoners, was summoned to the Parliament which was called by the barons in the King's name as Baron de Ros, 14 December 1264. When Alfred Lord Stourton was presenting his case in 1877, his Counsel referred to the parliament summoned by Simon de Montfort in this way. 'The parliament of the 49th of Henry III, although called in the King's name, was in reality called by Symon de Montfort, Earl of Leicester, while he detained the King as his prisoner, and the only peers summoned to it were those who espoused the earl's cause against the King.' In other words a phoney parliament. This view of things was accepted eventually by the House of Lords. But it has not prevented 28 generations bearing the honoured name of de Ros from sitting in the House of Lords. We will take up the story of the fortunes of some of these noble houses again in Interlude III.

CHAPTER III

1603–1642

Emergence and Dismissal

The seventeenth century was to see a fundamental re-distribution of political power in Britain. By the end of the century the King's position would be far weaker though still highly significant, that of Parliament far stronger. Different views may be held as to how far Charles I was seeking to establish a degree of autocracy beyond that of the Tudors. His conception of his royal prerogative was doomed. With wiser counsels on his part or on that of his opponents, could the readjustment have been effected without civil war?

In the mortal struggle between the King and the House of Commons, it is difficult to pin down the influence exerted by the House of Lords. In the years before the Civil War they were an incalculable force. The time was to come when the Civil War divided the peers sharply into a minority who backed Parliament and a majority who backed the King, actively or otherwise. The House was abolished by the fiat of the House of Commons in 1649, soon after the execution of the King. It came back very much its old self in 1660.

In the first 40 years of the seventeenth century the number of peers had much increased. Queen Elizabeth had been chary of creating peers. At the time of her death there were fewer peers than at the time of her accession. There were in fact only 52 lay lords. James went ahead fast with the creation and, as time went on, with the sale of peerages to raise extra revenue. The English peerage was increased by December 1628 to 126 (bishops included). Charles in the last seven years of his life resumed the practice of selling titles. But the Civil War sharply reduced the number of Lords who attended at Westminster. Already before it began in 1642, the King had given his assent to a Bill for the exclusion of the bishops. In 1646 a parliamentary ordinance declared that all titles conferred since May 1642 were null and void. By this time there were only 29 qualified to vote. Attendance was often less than 20, but they still had their honourable moments (see below).

Drawing heavily on Elizabeth Read-Foster's *House of Lords 1603– 1949, Structure, Procedure and the Nature of its Business*, we can obtain an excellent picture of the House during this period, roughly halfway between the date of its formation and the present time. Then, as now, the Lords were expected to maintain a certain standard of conduct, but they seemed to find it harder to achieve in those days. Today we are sometimes told that we are over-courteous to each other by carrying our words of respect to the point of absurdity. Speaking for myself, I would not have it otherwise or yearn for some of the encounters in the early seventeenth century.

In February 1621, the Earl of Berkshire, when he entered the House, violently thrust aside Lord Scrope who had preceded him. The House took the gravest view of the offence. The Earl was deprived of his sword and committed a close prisoner to the Fleet prison 'that posterity might take the more notice thereof '. When the Earl committed suicide some years later, there were those who believed he never recovered from this humiliation, but Simonds D'Ewes, who described him as a violent and disappointed man, ascribed his death to other causes.

In 1620 Lord Spencer cast aspersions on the ancestor of the Earl of Arundel. Arundel retorted that his forebears suffered for king and country while Spencer's were tending sheep. The Bishop of Coventry and Lichfield attempted to heal the breach by remarking that 'it is no disgrace to be called a shepherd'. Eventually both lords submitted themselves to the censure of the House and the Clerk removed their words of altercation from the record. It is rare today that the Standing Order against an asperity in speech is read to the House, though I heard it done not long ago. The establishment of the Order apparently resulted from a sharpness of speech which was reported to the House in 1626.

In 1641 during the debate on the Strafford Bill of Attainder the Earl of Pembroke struck Lord Maltravers (heir to the Earl of

Arundel – that name again) with his white staff. Maltravers hurled an inkstand at Pembroke but fortunately missed. Both submitted to the House upon their knees – where people seemed to find themselves more often those days. When the Earl of Warwick began to speak on a point of religion the Archbishop of York cried, 'Hold your tongue' and refused to withdraw until forced to do so. And plenty of other illustrations could be provided from that more hot-tempered age.

The ceremony of the opening of Parliament under the early Stuarts was marked by a magnificent procession. First came trumpeters on horseback, then heralds in full dress. Next on horseback and on foot came the gentlemen of the law. The peers in their scarlet robes and the bishops followed. First the barons, then the viscounts, then the earls, with the two archbishops. Two gentlemen ushers, one of the Black Rod, walked before the Prince of Wales. The King on a superb white horse was brilliantly dressed in a crimson velvet cape, lavishly trimmed and lined with ermine. He wore a lace ruff; his jacket and breeches were white. On his head was a jewelled crown and he carried an unsheathed sword in his right hand, point upwards. Gentlemen pensioners with halberds surrounded him. Is it all so very different from what we see today on such occasions as the coronation?

The King usually attended the House for the opening of Parliament. He returned usually on the second day for the presentation of the Commons Speaker and once more at the close of a parliament to receive the subsidy and give his answer to Bills. Usually he sent messages to the House by the Presiding Officer, the Lords of the Privy Council or in 1621 or 1624 by the Prince. In 1621 he spoke concerning patents and monopolies. In 1641 Charles addressed the House on behalf of Strafford. More often he addressed both Houses or delegations from both Houses at Whitehall.

The King had wide powers of influencing the House through his ability to create peers and his right to nominate archbishops and bishops. He was said to have created five new barons in 1641 in an attempt to save Strafford. He sometimes declined to issue a Writ of Summons to a peer or a spiritual lord. This, however, was an exceptional tactic. An hereditary peer had by this time established the right to be summoned. Indeed, the King and the House were both concerned with enforcing attendance. In James's first two Parliaments in 1606 and 1614 the House levied a fine on members absent without leave but fines and threats were not to much avail. Attendance in the years 1621–1629 was rarely higher than 60 and very often less. In 1642 the King called on his subjects to depart from Westminster and to attend him at Hampton Court, York, but the House refused to honour such arrangements. One of the features which passed away a century ago was the system of proxies. When the King granted a member of the Upper House a licence to be absent from Parliament he also gave him the right to nominate a proxy.

The House usually sat in the morning, convening at nine o'clock and rising before noon. Occasionally the nine was advanced to eight and once, during the summer of 1641, to six. There was one occasion when the House sat until eleven in the evening, but this was quite exceptional. Indeed it is not common today.

The Presiding Officer, the Lord Chancellor or Lord Keeper, was both spokesman for the Crown and servant of the House. The Clerk was a figure modest in his black barrister's gown and yet of much significance. He sat on a woolsack facing the Presiding Officer. He and the Presiding Officer were always present when the House was in session. Both had assisted in preparing the agenda. A major responsibility of the Clerk was to record the proceedings in the House and to prepare an account of the decisions of Parliament in the Parliament Roll. His record was the official record of the King's Parliament.

There is an abiding interest in the role of the Lord Chancellor or Lord Keeper described above as both spokesman for the Crown and servant of the House. The House of Lords today is it would seem the only assembly in the world whose proceedings are not controlled by a chairman or a speaker. The Speaker of the House of Commons would certainly regard himself as a servant of the House. Nevertheless he maintains order and in that sense is in control. The House of Lords prides itself today on being self-governing. There is no one individual who is empowered for example to call a speaker to order. Insofar as it falls to anyone's responsibility it falls to the Leader of

59

the House or whoever happens to be the senior figure on the government's front bench. But it is open to any individual member to intervene for such a purpose.

The Standing Orders of the House of Lords, first drawn up in 1621, provided that the Lord Chancellor 'is not to adjourne the House or doe anything els, as mouth of the House, without the consent of the Lords first had excepting the ordinarie things about Bills, which are of course, wherein, the Lords may likewise overrule, as for preferring one Bill before another, and such like.' The Lord Chancellor or Lord Keeper, seated at the main Woolsack at one end of the House, nevertheless carried a responsibility for making sure that the business of the House flowed smoothly. That is a delicate responsibility, as I know well today from having been Leader myself and served under a dozen Leaders. Very seldom is the authority of the Leader flouted providing always that he remembers to describe himself as servant of the House. On one occasion the late Lord Stansgate persisted to the point when the Leader of the day, Lord Hailsham, had to warn him, 'I have my remedy.' 'Oh,' said the octogenarian Stansgate, 'if the noble Lord has his remedy, he had better use it.' Whereupon the noble Lord, Lord Hailsham, moved and carried a motion 'that the noble Lord, Lord Stansgate, be no longer heard' (my recollection).

The Gentleman Usher of the Black Rod was generally responsible for order about the House. 'During the sitting of parliament, Black Rod was generally responsible for order about the House and its surroundings. When Old Palace Yard became too crowded or noisy, he was authorised to clear out a canvas "tent or booth lately erected". To keep out carts and waggons, he hired one Charles Best to tend a chain to block the way. He was in charge of and probably appointed the groom porters (20d *per diem*), the door-keepers, the waiters, the messengers and pursuivants, all of them assisted him in his work.' (Elizabeth Read-Foster)

His chief duty was the care and custody of the doors of the High Court of Parliament. On several occasions he was ordered to inform all lords in London that the King commanded their presence in Parliament. When a lord was introduced the Gentleman Usher and the Garter King of Arms led the little procession into the Chamber.

He summoned the Commons to the Bar of the Upper House to hear the King or to hear a judgement of the Lords. He sought and brought to the House those who offended against its privileges. His post was considered to be a lucrative one. He received an allowance of 5 shillings for each day the House sat for himself and his men. At the end of a session he could take desks, tables, cupboards, etc. for his own purposes. However, it appears that he went too far when he tried to appropriate 'the timberwork of the Court made for the trial of the Earl of Strafford.' He received a share of the fees, for example on the first entrance of a peer into Parliament, or on the translation of a bishop from one see to another.

It is only possible here to mention one other group of officers. Curiously enough the judges were regarded as assistants. They were indeed summoned by Writs of Assistance. In the reign of Edward I and for many years afterwards, they had been full members of the parliament, but by the seventeenth century they were regarded as assistants to the peers and prelates. In theory they were summoned to assist the King. They sat in the middle of the Parliament chamber and remained bare-headed until the Lords gave them leave to cover. They did not speak unless required to do so. The unqualified ruled supreme – a far cry from today.

Much work has been done in recent years on the growth of a political opposition to the House of Lords in the first half of the seventeenth century. It has long been recognised that the emergence of an opposition party in the House of Commons played a large part in altering the balance of power within the government of England. It now seems to be accepted that the Opposition nobles also exercised considerable influence. There is no doubt that they attained control of their House during the two critical parliamentary sessions of 1626 and 1628. The previous dominance of the Crown over that House was seriously shaken. To quote Professor Jess Stoddart Flemion: 'When the Crown lost the certain loyalty of the peerage, the last remnant of traditional parliamentary management upon which the Stuart monarchy depended for its precariously balanced authority, had been destroyed.'

It is almost impossible in telling our tale to keep the political and the judicial functions of the House of Lords apart, as we shall see when we come to the trial of Strafford. For the moment, however, let us attempt to concentrate on the former.

The 'popular peers' raised the first complaint over the sales of titles of nobility. They provided the leadership in every clash between the House of Lords and the Crown concerning royal control over the deliberations of that body. It was the investigation started by them which contributed to the resumption of judicial authority in the House of Lords – 'The greatest expansion of constitutional authority for the Upper House since its inception.' (Jess Stoddart Flemion). The new Standing Committees became dominated by Opposition peers. These committees, the Committee for Customs and the Committee for Petitions, played a crucial role in Opposition victories and in the expansion of the influence of the House. The greatest constitutional debate of the decade led in 1628 to the passage of the Petition of Right. The Crown had expected that this measure, coming from the Commons, would be easily defeated in the Lords, but found instead 'its representatives out-debated and out-manoeuvred at every turn' (Jess Stoddart Flemion).

It seems that the dissident peers belonged to no single category, although sympathy for Presbyterian religious views seems to be a prominent factor. One tie bound these men together – 'a deep and continuous desire to express their disapproval of Stuart government.' From 1629 to 1640 Charles I ruled without a parliament, but during this period an aristocratic network of political friends, relations, patrons and clients had been working out their programme. Clarendon in his history has named the leaders of this grouping: 'In the Lords House the Earls of Essex, Bedford, Warwick, the Lords Saye and Kimbolton were the governing voices, attended by Brooke, Wharton, Paget and such like. In the House of Commons, Mr Pym, Mr Hampden, Mr St John, Mr Holles and Mr Fiennes absolutely governed, being stoutly seconded upon all occasions by Mr Strode, Sir John Hotham . . . Sir Walter Earle, young Sir Henry Vane and many others of the same tempers and dispositions.'

Professor Paul Christianson in a learned essay: *The Peers, The People and Parliamentary Management in the First Six Months of the Long Parliament,* has been at pains to analyse the various degrees of subordination represented by the relationship between patron and client. He says for example that 'great differences of wealth and prestige such as those between the Earl of Bedford and John Pym made for a relationship of full clientage.' Whether or not this is accepted by all admirers of Pym, it provides us with an excuse for pausing for a while over the Earl of Bedford in question. Georgiana Blakiston in her *Woburn and the Russells* brings him vividly before us: 'Van Dyck's great portrait of the 4th Earl of Bedford depicts a man who appears careworn indeed, though not oppressed by uncertainties; rather one who, sustained by steady beliefs and strict principles, is strong in the knowledge that his life has not been wasted in idleness and frivolity. It is evident that he has no use for the gaudy trappings of nobility – plainness is all. Cast in the Protestant mould he stands every inch a Puritan in sober black garments without so much as a border of lace to his deep white collar.'

He rebuilt Woburn Abbey and made it the principal home of the family; he carried out the improvement and development of the Covent Garden estate, tentatively begun by his predecessors; and he was the chief promoter of a scheme for draining the fens in the counties of Cambridge and Huntingdon; the reclaimed area, when the work was completed by his son, becoming known as the Bedford Level. But we are concerned with his role in national politics. Early in the reign of Charles I (1625) he had been sent down into Devonshire of which county he was Lord Lieutenant and detained there until the end of the session as a mark of the King's disapproval of his subscription of the Petition of Right. He was one of the sternest opponents of the increasing power of the Crown and a strong upholder of the rule of Parliament. Georgiana Blakiston described Pym as having risen to prominence under Bedford's patronage. (But the reader should turn to the present Lord Russell's *Parliament and English Politics 1621–1629* for another view of these years.)

The Judicial Role of the House of Lords

Some retracing of steps is necessary when we come to the judicial functions of the House of Lords. Today when we talk of a decision being reached by the House of Lords as the supreme tribunal in this country we are referring to a decision taken by five law lords. The other 1,100 members of the House including myself have as little to do with it as the man in the street but originally, of course, it was totally different.

In the beginning was the old *curia regis* in which judicial and legislative functions were combined. Gradually the various courts of justice separated themselves from the old *curia regis*. I will leave over for a moment the jurisdiction of the Lords in cases of impeachment by the Commons and in the trials of peers. With regard to other matters the Lords gradually lost all original jurisdiction, except in certain questions relating to the peerage, though, in the end, they retained the power of giving a final decision upon writs of error or appeals from courts below (Pike: *Constitutional History of the House of Lords*).

By the time of Charles I the judicial role of the Lords was much diminished. Now came a notable revival. The word revolutionary has been applied to the expansion of this role in the first half of the century. In Elizabeth's reign and the years 1603 to 1621 the House of Lords judged no cases of impeachment. It heard a few cases of error from the King's Bench but no appeal from other sources. It accepted no cases of first instance, except those that affected its own privileges. In 1621 and the years following, however, impeachment cases at times became the chief business of the House. Meanwhile the House accepted a wide variety of cases of the first instance. 'Judicial hearings occupied a major portion of the Lords' time. The High Court of Parliament became a working reality.' (Elizabeth Read-Foster). After the Restoration the Lords never got back their previous range of powers.

It is hard to know whether the proceedings on impeachment and still more, those involved in the Bill of Attainder, should be called

64

political or judicial. The same would sometimes at least be true of the trial of peers by peers. Those who could vote in all these cases were almost all legally unqualified.

In some ways the most remarkable of all these trials was that of Francis Bacon, Viscount St Alban. The House of Commons was concerned to present the evidence it had against Bacon to the Lords 'without prejudice' being fully conscious that Bacon was not only a peer but Lord Chancellor and custodian of the Great Seal. At a conference between the two Houses, the Commons informed the Lords of abuses in the Courts of Justice and accused the Lord Chancellor of 'great bribery and corruption'. The Lords moved to investigate the case. Bacon had a private audience with the King. He asked for the particulars of the charge against him. Where his answers were 'fair and clear', he wished to extenuate the charge; and where no answer was possible and the proofs were full and undeniable, he declared that he would confess and put himself on the mercy of the Lords. The King made no answer but referred him to the Upper House. In the end Bacon did not defend himself but confessed to every point except one. The House sent the Gentleman Usher and the Serjeant armed with the Mace to bid Bacon come to hear judgement. On the appointed day he failed to appear. (It should be mentioned that he had not been previously required to appear because of his position as Lord Chancellor.) The House of Lords voted that Bacon was guilty and determined his sentence. They informed the House of Commons that they were ready to give judgement if members of the Commons with their Speaker would come to demand it. The Lords put on their robes, the Commons duly appeared and the Lord Chief Justice as presiding officer of the Upper House pronounced the judgement and sentence. This consisted of:

1 A fine and ransom of £40,000
2 Imprisonment in the Tower during the King's Pleasure
3 To be incapable of any office or employment, in the state, or commonwealth
4 That he shall never sit in Parliament.

3 May 1621

In the event these penalties were much mitigated.

The trial of the Earl of Bristol in 1626 has always interested students of the period. The case was initiated by the King in a letter sent to the House of Lords. He requested the Lords to summon the Earl as a delinquent to answer to offences committed in Spain and England. The House debated at length whether he should be sent for and answer in his place as a peer, or remain in the custody of the Gentleman Usher. Finally they ordered that the Gentleman Usher should bring Bristol to the Bar and that Bristol should 'kneel at his coming, in respect he is accused of High Treason'. When the charge was being read out, Bristol interrupted and reminded the House that he had previously petitioned in a similar fashion against the Duke of Buckingham. He asked not to be 'impeached' until his charge of so high a nature be first heard. Eventually the House agreed to hear the King's charge against the Earl and then the Earl's charge against the Duke. The proceedings continued, great care being taken by the House that the accusation of treason against Bristol should not invalidate Bristol's accusation against Buckingham. But neither case proceeded to trial because the King dissolved Parliament before that could happen.

No apology is needed in any account of the House of Lords in the seventeenth century for dwelling on the trial of Strafford. We must bear in mind throughout that Charles I held a view of his own prerogative which was opposed to that of many if not most of his leading subjects. At one point he addressed the Commons in this way: 'Remember that parliaments are altogether in my power for their calling, sitting and dissolution. Therefore as I find them good or evil, they are to continue to be or not to be.' He governed for eleven years without Parliament. Today it is a meaningless question to ask whether this was legal or illegal. In the same way one cannot connect the sentencing and execution of Strafford with any legal process.

The Earl of Strafford

The career of Thomas Wentworth, Earl of Strafford (1593–1641) must be briefly recalled. By 1621, aged 28, he was making his mark in Parliament. He was soon playing a distinctive role, associating with those who objected to arbitrary taxation and imprisonment, but at the same time jealous of the prerogatives of the Crown. Created Baron Wentworth in 1628, he came down heavily on the side of the King when the latter dissolved Parliament and ruled without it for eleven years.

Strafford travelled to Dublin in 1633 to take up the position of Lord Deputy of Ireland. In that capacity his motto was 'thorough'. An alternative description would have been to call it an arbitrary despotism. No doubt this prime consideration was to save money for the British treasury by ruthless efficiency. It is argued that he made genuine efforts to protect the poor from the exactions of the rich.

By 1639 he was back in England as the King's Chief Counsellor and in November of that year was created Earl of Strafford, but he would not enjoy that title for long. He had been in favour of calling Parliament together in 1640, but he was soon in great difficulties. The King supported his request for money to pay for war against the Scots. But Parliament had no stomach for such operations. The Short Parliament was dissolved, although a new House of Commons was no better from the point of view of the King and Strafford. The majority of the new parliament passionately believed that the King, Strafford and Archbishop Laud were involved in a conspiracy not only to organise an absolute monarchy, but to subject the country to the Papacy. They were determined to bring down Strafford and Laud. Strafford asked permission to stay at his post in York where he was Commander-in-Chief of the army, but the King felt the need of him at his side in London. He travelled to London in November 1640, well aware of the grave perils confronting him, but trusting it would seem that his peers would refuse to condemn him. Pym thought that the moment had come to strike. The doors of the House were locked. A Select Committee was named for a con-

67

ference with the Lords 'and the charge against the Earl of Strafford'. Strafford was on his way to the House, but Pym got there first. He informed their Lordships that the Commons of England impeached the Earl of Strafford, Lord Lieutenant of Ireland, of High Treason.

The Lords had expected no less and agreed to consider the charge while Pym withdrew. Strafford came hastening towards his place in the Chamber, but a cry arose among the benches: 'Withdraw, withdraw'. With 'a proud, glooming countenance' he moved on while the cry grew louder and some of the peers rose to their feet to stop him. He stood still, asking for an explanation. Pym's message was read to him and the Lord Keeper told him he must withdraw pending the Lords' decision. Slowly he turned and retraced his steps.

After ten minutes he was called back. He was brought to the Bar and told to kneel. He obeyed in silence and the Earl of Manchester read to him the formal intimation of the Commons' charge. He learnt that he was to be sequestered from the House and placed in confinement until the hearing of the cause. Rising, he protested against the unprecedented severity of this measure and asked leave to speak. Manchester informed him that he could reach the ear of the Lords only by petition. Slowly he moved away, bareheaded and stooping between the long lines of his peers, seeing no one, saluting no one.

We are concerned only with the procedure, not the issues. It seems today astonishing that he should be confined during the hearing of the court with no serious argument presented for or against him. Members of Parliament were forbidden to visit him without licence; a request for bail was refused. Thirteen days after his arrest on 24 November 1640, Pym placed the articles of Strafford's impeachment before the House of Commons. On the following morning they were submitted to the Lords. That same afternoon Strafford was brought to hear them. He asked at the end if he might have time to consider his answer and leave to consult counsel and to call witnesses. Such questions, he was informed, could only be decided on petition. He was confined to three rooms only in the Tower and submitted to other humiliating restrictions. I need not continue a detailed analysis of the trial, dramatic though it was. Sir Thomas Knydett was not well disposed to a prisoner whom the prosecution had 'laid open to see so foul a man' but he could not withhold a tribute; 'I think that there was never any man of so unmovable a temper, for in all this time, although his provocations sometimes have been great, yet he hath not discovered the least passion, but when he speaks he doth it with so much bravery and modest courtship of both the houses and in such language as begets admiration in all the beholders, especially in a business where he can make good clear work for himself.'

Most of the peers had no legal qualifications whatever. They were not well disposed towards Strafford as can be seen from the humiliations already described and as was to become evident later on. But impeachment was supposed to be a judicial process with forms of law observed, and the Commons realised that they were not succeeding.

At this juncture, the Earl of Bedford might have played a crucial part. There was a moment when reconciliation seemed possible. Bedford was deeply imbued with progressive principles but he began to consider that the Crown and the Lords should stand together against the populace to prevent terrible disaster. He and Hertford joined Bristol and Savile in an attempt to preserve the life of Strafford. The King in the early part of 1641 showed himself anxious to obtain the support of some of the popular leaders and especially the popular peers. He began by making seven of the peers Privy Councillors, viz. Bristol, Bedford, Essex, Hertford, Saye, Mandeville and Savile (19 February 1641). Some of the popular peers were even given office, for example Holland, Saye and Essex. Savile was promised the Presidency of the Council of the North while it was understood that Bedford was to be Lord Treasurer and Mandeville, soon to be Earl of Manchester, Lord Privy Seal. Professor Firth, in his authoritative book *The House of Lords during the Civil War* (published in 1910) is disparaging about the King's intentions: 'The King was not prepared to give these new officers any real influence over his policy. Their appointment therefore led to no lasting result.' He admits that the death of Bedford removed a man 'whose influence might have made the plan the basis of a reconciliation.'

Bedford was in any case having much difficulty in moderating the violent opinion of some of his peers. The Earl of Essex was adamant: 'stone dead has no fellow'. A few days later Bedford took to his bed with a fatal illness which soon emerged as smallpox. Clarendon wrote of Bedford: 'He would have proposed and advised moderate courses but was not incapable, for want of resolution, of being carried into violent ones, if his advice were not submitted to.'

It seems possible to arrive at a kinder opinion, which makes his death all the more tragic.

As Professor Firth has pointed out, to the Lords the question of Strafford's guilt or innocence was a judicial question, which must be legally proved and the accused was entitled to certain definite rights. To the Commons, the question was a political one. Strafford was a danger to the nation and his capital punishment necessary to its safety. There was no pretence of fair play.

On 10 April 1641 an open breach between the Houses took place. The managers of the accusation wished to offer fresh evidence. Strafford very reasonably asked to be allowed to offer fresh evidence too. The Lords decided that both sides should be given permission. But this was quite unacceptable to the Commons. The Commons, says Robert Baillie in his book *Letters*: 'The Commons on both sides of the House, rose in a fury, with a shout of "Withdraw, withdraw, withdraw," get all to their feet, on with their hats, cocked their beavers in the King's sight. We did all fear it should go to a present tumult. They went all away in confusion; Strafford slipped away to his barge, and to the Tower, glad to be gone lest he should be torn to pieces; the King went home in silence; the Lords to their House.'

The Commons now resorted to what Veronica Wedgwood has called 'the antiquated and terrible machinery of the Bill of Attainder'. The Bill was duly pushed through the House of Commons. The pathetic vacillations of Charles I who had promised not to let Strafford die need not concern us here. A landslide of timidity had begun in the Lords.

A contemporary pamphlet gives some idea of the pressure of the mob. 'The people being inflamed again by the King's speech, came to Westminster with the number of five or six thousand, having weapons and battoons in their hands; at the entering of every coach some cried Justice others Execution, a third man told his fellows that both were to be conjoined, and that Justice and Execution was the noble word; upon which (*quasi dato signo*) all the rabble cried aloud with one voice Justice and Execution, with a wonderful strange noise; some went to the coach sides, and told the Lords that they must and would have justice done upon the Deputy.'

The whole bench of bishops persuaded themselves that they were disqualified from voting. In a thin House, on 7 May 1641, the Bill of Attainder was passed by 26 votes to 19. The King continued to vacillate, praying and hesitating. One is ready to believe that his final surrender was to preserve his wife and children from the howling mob. He gave his consent to the Bill – and never forgave himself. Even to the moment when he himself mounted the scaffold, with awe-inspiring courage.

A few sentences from his *Reflection upon the Death of Strafford* can be quoted: 'I never met with a more unhappy conjuncture of affairs than in the [case] of that unfortunate earl; when between my own unsatisfiedness in conscience, and a necessity (as some told me) of satisfying the importunities of some people; I was persuaded by those that I think wished me well, to choose rather what was safe, than what seemed just; preferring the outward peace of my kingdoms with men, before that inward exactness of conscience before God.'

Charles went on to say that he had not intended to employ him 'in my affairs against the advice of my parliament'. 'But I would not,' he wrote, 'have had any hand in his death of whose guiltlessness I was better assured than any man living could be.' Charles, later to become a martyr in the Church of England, would have been gratified by the Act passed in 1661 which reversed the Attainder. After some sharp remarks about the 'turbulent party responsible for the outrage' the new Act declared that 'the Act for the Attainder of Thomas Earl of Strafford had good reasons for expecting justice' or at least mercy from his colleagues in the House of Lords. Professor Timmins of Alabama University, produced in 1974 a searching monograph on the trial and execution of Strafford, including a careful analysis of the reasons for the outcome. It is not necessary to agree with his estimate of the sharp decline in the prestige of the peers in the preceding years. There is no doubt, however, that MPs had come to regard their House as the much more important body. John Pym described the Lords as merely 'a third estate by inheritance and birthright'. Others took up the same theme: 'This House being the representative body of the whole kingdom and their lordships being but particular persons and coming to parliament in a particular capacity.' Be that as it may, it is obvious that the Lords were by this time living on a knife edge and were only too well aware of the fact.

Timmins' analysis of the voting of Strafford's attainder is fascinating. What is known is that there were 147 peers and of this number less than a third (45) were present, which suggests considerable timidity on the part of the majority. Only 19, we know, voted for Strafford. Who were they? The question, as Timmins admits, 'is highly conjectural'. However he believes that he has identified 13 of the 19 and he concludes that the only lords who voted for Strafford were his friends and connections, or else the most steadfast adherents of the Crown. 'He was unable to appeal to the other lords who required stronger reasons than justice to come out for him amid so much danger.'

Archbishop Laud

The execution of Strafford was rounded off by an execution two years later of his illustrious ally, the Archbishop of Canterbury, William Laud. By this time the Civil War was raging, the House of Lords had been reduced to an unimpressive rump of 12–16 members. We shall find in a moment, however, that they were capable of one dying act of courage before their liquidation (for the time being).

Hugh Trevor-Roper, now Lord Dacre of Glanton, published a

life of Laud in 1940. For quality of treatment it is not likely to be surpassed. Twenty-one years later Trevor-Roper, then Regius Professor of History at Oxford, wrote a new preface to a later edition. He reckoned that if he were writing at that time he would probably be more sympathetic to Laud and less sympathetic to his ideals.

We can take up the story when Strafford (still Wentworth) arrived back in England in September 1639. By this time Trevor-Roper considers that Laud's political influence had reached an end. For six years he had been fighting a losing battle, seeking by the exercise of despotic authority and backstairs influence to establish a form of responsible autocracy: and he had failed.

It has been said before now that the religious system that Laud was seeking to impose was in fact adopted after the Restoration. Trevor-Roper, in his recent book of essays *Catholics, Anglicans and Puritans* sums up magisterially: 'It was not Laudianism that ruined Charles I but Charles I who ruined Laudianism.' Charles was now persuaded to recall Parliament after a gap of 11 years. The financial requirements of war against Scotland rendered it inevitable. The Short Parliament was soon dissolved but the Long Parliament was no more comfortable to the King and his advisers. Strafford and Laud were bound to be the principal targets. Strafford faced his accusers boldly, confident that he could turn the tables on them. Laud exhibited a spirit of Christian resignation.

On 18 December 1640 both parties began proceedings against him. The message of the House of Commons was taken to the Lords. Laud was formally impeached of high treason. He spoke a few words in his defence amid interruptions, we are told, from the Presbyterian peers, for he then withdrew and was summoned back to kneel like Strafford at the Bar. Then he was delivered over to the custody of Maxwell (Usher of the Black Rod), again like Strafford. He was allowed to go to Lambeth to collect books and papers necessary for his defence. 'I stayed at Lambeth till the evening,' he entered in his diary, 'to avoid the gazing of the people. I went to evening prayer in my chapel. The psalms of the day and chapter 50 of Isaiah gave me great comfort. God make me worthy of it and fit to receive it. As I went to my barge, hundreds of my poor neighbours stood there and prayed for my safety and return to my house: for which I bless God and them.' His apparent arrogance had been superseded by an edifying humility. After ten weeks he was transferred to the Tower where Strafford was also prisoner, though they were not allowed to meet. The final communication between him and Strafford is historic.

The night before his execution Strafford sent a message to Laud asking for his prayers that night, and for his appearance at his window next morning, to give Strafford his blessing on his way to the scaffold. Laud promised to do both these things. Next morning, as Strafford passed underneath, Laud came to the window. Strafford bowed himself to the ground: 'My Lord,' said he, 'your prayers and blessing.' The Archbishop lifted up his hands and bestowed both, but fainted away, overcome with grief. Strafford proceeded a little further and bowed a second time saying, 'Farewell my Lord, God protect your innocency.' Laud, ashamed of his weakness in fainting at the critical moment, declared that he hoped that, when his own execution came, 'the world should perceive that he had been more sensible of the Lord Strafford's loss than his own.' His hope would in due course be granted.

He was not brought to trial until he had been imprisoned for nearly two years. Meanwhile he had been exposed to a whole series of humiliations. On 31 May 1643 he was aroused from bed at four o'clock in the morning by the fanatical Puritan, William Prynne, and a search party. Prynne's desire for revenge was understandable. In the days of Laud's ascendancy he had had his ears cropped and been thrown into prison. He made the most of his present opportunity of getting his own back. The Archbishop was still in bed; Prynne at once set about riffling through his pockets and, before he left, had removed many documents which he judged, not incorrectly, would be useful to the prosecution. In particular, he took away Laud's spiritual diary which he then proceeded to edit and distort in shameful fashion.

When the trial eventually took place the same situation arose as with Strafford. It was impossible to make out a legal case for impeachment. Laud defended himself with much less vehemence but just as ably as Strafford. Once again, therefore, the Commons were driven to adopt the non-judicial method of an Act of Attainder. This was inevitably passed by the Commons and sent up to the Lords. 'There for a while it stuck; the Lords, even in their attenuated condition, were still mindful of their judicial capacity, or at least of their dignity and independence, now the more valued since it was but a shadow.' (Trevor-Roper). But the Commons were not to be denied; they threatened the Lords with mob violence unless they hastened to pass the required ordinance. They attempted to preserve their dignity by proposing a conference which took place on 2 January 1645. The Commons disclaimed all intention of being bound by Statute. Laud, if necessary, could be made guilty by ordinance. The Lords felt that it was hopeless; the ordinance was duly passed. The brutality of the Commons towards Laud is sickening to read about. Laud requested that he suffer death by the axe instead of by hanging. The Lords agreed, the Commons rejected the request without a division. Ultimately, however, it was granted.

Laud met his end with edifying resignation.

CHAPTER IV

1642–1660

The Years Between

The Civil War which began in 1642 saw Charles I summoning the peers to York and the parliamentarians requesting their continued presence at Westminster. It is estimated that perhaps half of the peers supported Charles more or less actively, a quarter supported the parliamentarians and the other quarter were either unable or unwilling to take sides. At least one peer, the Earl of Bedford, as has been seen, fought for both.

The Lord Derby of the day removed any suggestions of time-serving that might have clung to the family after the famous 'switch' at Bosworth. He performed heroic deeds on behalf of the King. He was reckoned, however, when captured, to be not a prisoner of war but a traitor, and was executed as such. 'Among the sufferers for King Charles I none cast greater lustre on the cause.'

The number of lords functioning at Westminster was reduced to very small figures. The period indeed from 1642 to the Restoration in 1660 constitutes a break in the long continuity of the House. Nevertheless the residue who continued at Westminster revealed an independent courage at a crucial moment.

On 1 January 1649 the House of Commons passed an ordinance for the trial of King Charles and a resolution setting up a Court of Commissioners for that purpose. On the next day, the measures were sent up to a House of perhaps twelve peers. A present member of the House of Lords is entitled to feel proud of the reaction of his predecessors. Not one of them had a word to say in favour of the ordinance. Pembroke alone remained silent. The others denounced the ordinance in contemptuous terms. Derby said he would rather be torn to pieces than sit in such a judgement. The House then adjourned for a week in the despairing hope that the House of Commons would not be able to proceed without them.

The House of Commons responded firmly and decisively. They resolved that 'the Commons of England in parliament assembled, do Declare, That the People are, under God, the Original of all just Power. And do also Declare that the Commons of England, in Parliament assembled being chosen by, and representing the People, have the Supreme Power in the Nation. And do also Declare, That whatsoever is enacted, or declared the Law, by the Commons in parliament assembled, hath the Force of Law, and all the people of this Nation are concluded thereby, although the Consent and concurrence of King, or House of Peers, be not had thereunto.'

The House of Lords was not automatically abolished, but their *raison d'être* was removed. Abolition was to follow on 19 March. The House of Commons then resolved: 'The Commons of England, assembled in Parliament, finding by too long experience that the House of Lords is useless and dangerous to be continued, have thought it fit to Ordain and Enact, and be it Ordained and Enacted by this present Parliament, and by the Authority of the same, That from henceforth the House of Lords in Parliament shall be and is wholly abolished and taken away.' The privileges of peers were thus abolished and so were the judicial functions of the House.

Cromwell, who had never been enthusiastic about the abolition of the Lords, conceived the idea of establishing a new-style House of Lords without bishops. After considerable argument with the Commons Writs of Summons to members of 'the other House', about 60 in number, were issued in 1657. Among those called were some who had been peers before the rebellion and some men of ancient family, more than one of whom obtained a peerage after the Restoration. The others were men who had rendered distinguished service to the Commonwealth or the Protector. Parliament met on 7 January 1658. After a dispute with the Commons, who objected to calling the other House the House of Lords, this parliament was dissolved by Cromwell. His son and successor in the Protectorate, Richard Cromwell, summoned a parliament including the members of 'the

77

Other House' to meet on 27 January 1659. But this parliament also was soon dissolved.

That was the end of 'the other House'.

By February 1660 it was certain that the monarchy would be restored. What was not clear was whether restrictions would be placed on the King and, for that matter, on the House of Lords. In the event, as will be seen, the King was in theory accorded total freedom. The restoration of the old House of Lords was brought about after prolonged diplomatic discussions led by the Earl of Manchester on behalf of the Lords with General Monck. The restored journal of the House indicated the beginning of a steady build-up. The peers began to filter in as the negotiations reached a successful conclusion. One disputed question was the admissibility of those peers who had taken the King's side during the war. This was disposed of. There came a point when all the lords whose peerages had been in existence before the war were accepted as members. The question of peers created by Charles I or Charles II since the outbreak of the Civil War was left undecided.

When the House resumed eleven peers were present: five earls, one viscount and five barons, here appearing under the title of Ds, i.e. Dominus or Lord. We read that 'Comes Manchester' was appointed by the House to be Speaker *pro tem*. It was ordered 'That Monday next be appointed to be kept by the House as a day of fasting and humiliation, for seeking and blessing from God by prayer upon the meeting of both Houses of Parliament, in order to a settlement of this nation: and the place to be the Abbey Church in Westminster for the peers: Wherein the House of Commons to be desired to do the like for their House.'

Arrangements were made for delivering the records of the House to John Browne, Clerk of Parliaments. George Monck was nominated and appointed by the House to be Captain General of all the land forces, the concurrence of the House of Commons to be desired therein.

A committee was appointed to write letters desiring the attendance of the peers whom it was thought appropriate to summon to the House. The request was in these terms:

My Lord,

I am commanded by the House of Peers hereby to signify their pleasures that you do repair to attend the House with what convenient speed you can.

And so I rest, Your Lordship's humble servant,

E. Manchester, Speaker *pro Tempore*

E. Nottingham	L. Dela Warr
E. Rutland	L. Montagu
L. North	L. Bruce

The emergence of the Earl of Manchester as Speaker of the House of Lords in 1660 leads me to mention the part played during these revolutionary times by him and his father. Sir Henry Montagu, first Earl of Manchester (1563–1642), was both a judge and a politician. He entered Parliament in 1601 at first taking the popular side. He is described however as turning to account several opportunities of ingratiating himself with the King. He was appointed King's Counsel in 1607, and later he became Chief Justice of the King's Bench. The case of greatest public interest which came before him was that of Sir Walter Raleigh against whom he made an award of execution in 1618.

He moved on to become Lord High Treasurer, paying apparently £20,000 for the office. Then he was sworn President of the Council, continued in that office by Charles and created Earl of Manchester in 1625. Later he became Lord Privy Seal. He was, we are told, one of Charles's most trusted advisers and local appellants. During part of 1642 he acted as Speaker of the House of Lords. It will be recalled, see page 68, that it was he before whom Strafford was compelled to kneel when he was informed that he had been impeached by the House of Commons. This would not strike one as compatible with his outstanding loyalty to Charles.

His son, the second Earl of Manchester (1602–1671), had an equally interesting career. While his father was still alive he, as a member of the House of Commons, signed the Petition of the Twelve Peers urging the King to call a parliament and indeed was one of those who presented it to Charles. In spite of his father's attachment to the King he became, when he entered the House of

79

Lords in 1642, an acknowledged leader of the popular and puritan party there. Succeeding his father in November 1642, he was among the few peers who remained with the parliament when war broke out. He achieved a considerable military position but was considered to be lacking in energy as a commander.

On 25 November 1644, Cromwell laid before the House of Commons a narrative charging Manchester with neglect and incompetence in the prosecution of the war. Manchester defended himself vigorously but was eventually forced to resign his commission. He stoutly opposed the Ordinance for the King's Trial in the House of Lords and retired from public life soon after.

Cromwell summoned him to sit in his Upper House in December 1657 but Manchester declined. He took an active part in bringing about the Restoration and, having become Speaker of the Lords, welcomed the King on his arrival.

CHAPTER V

1660–1783

Before 'The Golden Years' and after

With the Restoration of 1660, the two Houses of Parliament came back to life almost, though not quite, as though nothing had happened in the meantime. The question was still undecided when Charles returned whether peerages created by himself and his father would entitle their holders to membership of the House. Charles immediately announced a decision in their favour. The bishops were still absent from the new House, but they were brought back in the following year.

Charles II was addressed by the Speakers of both Houses of Parliament. The Earl of Manchester, before whose father Strafford had been forced to kneel when impeached by the Commons, began his address in a style which Antonia Fraser has described as 'almost ludicrously obsequious'. Professor Firth refers to it as 'eloquent': 'Dread Sovereign!' he cried, 'I offer no flattering titles but speak the words of truth: you are the desire of three kingdoms, the strength and stay of the tribes of the people, for the moderating of extremities, the reconciling of differences, the satisfying of all interests' – and much more to the same effect.

No one however had any clear idea as to the powers of Parliament and the King respectively under the new arrangements. On paper there were no restrictions whatever on the powers of the King. Equally, it was obvious to him and to everyone that he would only govern with the co-operation of Parliament and the goodwill of the community, as Antonia Fraser brings out clearly.

A constitutional development which in theory rather than in practice was of much significance took place in the early years of

Charles II's reign. 'Feudal tenure by military service, which was an anachronism under the Stuarts, and was abolished during the Commonwealth, rose again into a nominal existence with the restoration of Charles II, only to be finally extinguished immediately afterwards.' (Pike). Pike goes so far as to say that 'this radical change affected the peers in such a manner as to change completely their relation to the King and to the State in general.' Originally every baron and earl was a soldier and in theory bound to give his counsel to the sovereign. But now with the abolition of military tenure he was freed from the greater part of his obligations. This constitutional change confirmed what had been a practical relationship developing over the centuries.

The peers emerged in a powerful position. No commoner wore the Blue Ribband of the Garter. 'If honour went predominantly to the peers, so too went responsibility.' (Maxwell P. Schoenfeld). They occupied the key positions in the Privy Council which acted as Charles II's personal council in the early years of his reign. The Lord Lieutenancies and the Chancellorships of Oxford and Cambridge rested in their hands. They emerged very successfully from the new land settlement. All those who had lost lands by confiscation regained them promptly, sometimes less encumbered than they had been before the Civil War. The Earl of Derby did not receive back all the family estates but he was amply compensated elsewhere.

Charles II went his own way in many respects publicly and privately. In one vital area he was thwarted and indeed humiliated. He himself was remarkably enlightened by modern standards in his approach to religious toleration. He would have wished to have extended it to his non-Anglican subjects, whether they were Catholics or Dissenters. Married to a Catholic, he himself became one on his death-bed. But all this was quite unacceptable to Parliament throughout his reign. Religious intolerance has indeed been described as the curse of the period. When in 1661 the bishops returned to the House of Lords, the Crown and Government could depend on their support on all but religious issues. The majority of the bishops steadily opposed Charles's attempts at religious moderation.

In December 1662 Charles issued a Royal Declaration of Toleration. But Parliament would have none of it. His attempts to achieve the same result by means of a Bill giving power to the Crown to dispense with the Act of Uniformity was doomed to failure. Later in the reign, in 1678, an appalling figure called Titus Oates purported to uncover a Popish Plot – a monstrous fabrication. A Bill was passed through both Houses which debarred Catholics from sitting in either. The King weakly gave way; 35 victims of public hysteria were executed.

The House of Commons moved against Lord Strafford on the strength of perjured evidence. The House of Lords went along with them after a spectacular 'trial' in Westminster Hall. Strafford, a dear old man, wrote to his daughter, 'This is the last time that I shall write unto you. I pray God bless you. Your poor old father has this comfort, that he is totally innocent of what he is accused of.' Which was all too true.

Charles II did not reprieve Stafford. 'I sign,' he said, 'with tears in my eyes.' At least he remitted the horrible mutilation which was traditional in such cases. The House of Commons expressed their doubts as to whether the King had the right to grant even this remittance. One prefers the profound sense of guilt that Charles I felt on not reprieving Strafford to the absence, so it seems, of any similar sense of guilt in Charles II in the same situation. The House of Commons were quite remorseless in their anti-Catholicism. Their objective was the exclusion of James, now a recognised Roman Catholic, from the succession. An Exclusion Bill with that object in view was passed by the Commons but thrown out by the Lords. Their own attitude to Catholicism was not at all favourable, but they felt that a threat to an established institution was involved.

Charles had the last word in his long struggle with Parliament. He dissolved them in 1681 and governed without Parliament for the last four years of his reign.

In 1681, Sir John Reresby was informed by a certain 'great man' that there was no question of a parliament since those near the King had advised him to another way of ruling the kingdom. In the last years of his life he tried out this 'other way of ruling' and found that it suited him very well. The historian of the House of Lords must regard this as one of the low points in the long saga. Yet the next period, 1689–1750, has been described by learned writers as the most important in the history of the House of Lords and the 'golden age of the House'.

James II came, made what are always described as serious errors, and disappeared. In retrospect, it seems extraordinary that James, a devout Catholic, was allowed to mount the throne of a country where his religion was officially forbidden. The House of Lords must take some responsibility for making this possible. It was inevitable that James would seek to improve the status of his co-religionists, and equally inevitable that this would bring about his downfall.

The peers had looked after their own interests with notable skill during the Civil War. They had now regained their position at Westminster. Of the seven signatories of the invitation to William III four were peers, the fifth was the Bishop of London, the sixth and seventh were members of the great noble houses of Russell and Sidney. J. V. Beckett (*The Aristocracy in England 1660–1914*) sums up succinctly: 'The executive was increasingly dominated by leading members of the peerage. They in turn exercised increasing influence over the Commons. By 1760 England was effectively an oligarchy.'

The Lords are credited therefore with playing a significant part in the transfer of power from James II to William III and his wife, James's daughter Mary, in 1688. That is no doubt true of some of the great nobles, but collectively speaking the Lords were not won over easily to the new regime. On 28 January 1689 the Commons agreed that James II had broken the original contract between monarchy and people, 'abdicated the government and left the throne vacant'. The issue now passed to the House of Lords. A tense battle developed between the adherents of James II and those of William of Orange. James's supporters, even after losing the motion for a regency, were able to control the House until 6 February. They continued to stave off pressure from the Commons to agree that James had abdicated.

There were three groups vying for control of the House during this time: the Loyalists who remained loyal to James, the Williamites who adhered to the Prince of Orange and were ready to follow the

Commons in installing William and Mary jointly on the vacant throne, and the small group led by Danby, which supported Mary as James's sole and rightful successor.

The Lords resolved by 55 to 51 that James should be described as having 'deserted' and not 'abdicated'; by 54 to 53 they reasserted that the throne was not vacant. But outside pressures in the end broke the stalemate. William announced that he would settle for nothing less than the crown in his own right, with Mary as joint sovereign. Finally, the insertion of the word 'abdicated' was carried by 65 votes to 45. William and Mary were at last declared King and Queen.

One example of tension between the two Houses may be touched on. Henry, the seventh Duke of Norfolk, was for a long time restrained by the House of Lords from carrying a Bill which would enable him to divorce his unfaithful wife. Party politics intruded. Henry had conformed to the Church of England (contrary to the main political outlook of his family) and was a strong Whig while his wife and her father were Catholics suspected of Jacobitism. The Bill rejected in January 1695 was the second that Norfolk had brought in. The adultery of the Duchess was duly proved but the House of Lords threw out the Bill insisting that the proof must first be made out 'in a lower Court'.

One interesting feature of the vote in the Lords was the split between all the bishops created during the present reign who were in favour of the Bill and all the bishops created by the two former kings who were against it. Eventually Norfolk got his Bill through. It has been said (David Ogg: *England in the reigns of James II and William III*) that the enactment of this third Bill marked the beginning of the long process whereby the state took over the control of divorce from the Church.

Queen Anne

The story of the House of Lords during the reign of Queen Anne is of particular interest. Professor Geoffrey Holmes wrote a chapter about it 20 years ago in his book *British Politics in the Age of Anne* which may never perhaps be superseded. He insists that 'with a wealth of talent to enrich its debates the House of Lords was unquestionably supreme as a political forum throughout Anne's reign. Its prestige was already high in 1702, and it was higher still in 1714. But it was far more than a superior debating-shop. There were periods in every one of Anne's parliaments when the Upper House manifestly rivalled the Lower in real political importance; and in the Queen's last three years the House of Lords consistently attracted more attention and certainly absorbed more of the time and energies of the government than did the Commons.'

Professor Holmes is equally insistent that 'whatever the complexities of the body politic in the early years of the eighteenth century, its life-blood was the existence and conflict of two major parties.' The more, however, that one reads about this period, the more powerful appears to be the influence remaining in the hands of the Crown.

Queen Anne, though often referred to as a simple woman, embodied in political terms a number of contradictions. There was no doubt that she was Tory or at least preferred the Tories. Sarah Duchess of Marlborough with whom for a long time she was infatuated, said of Anne: 'She regarded the Whigs as not only republicans who hated the very shadow of royal authority but implacable enemies of the Church of England.' Gila Curtis in her masterly concise biography of Anne considers that this is going too far but admits that 'Anne certainly regarded them with great suspicion.' Whig support of Dissenters and their irreverent attitude towards the throne were quite enough to have set her family against them. On the other hand, Sarah herself was a fanatical Whig.

Moreover the Whigs were far more ardent in pursuing the war with France then taking place (see below). Anne, on the whole, went along with that attitude. Sarah's husband, Marlborough, became in due course the greatest British general of the century. So there was plenty to balance the natural Toryism of Queen Anne.

Three principles we are told had distinguished the Tory from the Whig before the Revolution. One was a belief, admittedly declining, in the divine hereditary right of kings and in non-resistance. This was opposed to the Whig theory of monarchy, which was based on 'consent' and assumed a right of resistance if the King ceased to command this consent. In 1679 the Whigs had been prepared to reject hereditary rights and some had been ready to resort to resistance in order to make sure that a Protestant, not the Catholic James, would succeed Charles II. A second integral part of the ideology of pre-Revolution Toryism was in Holmes' words 'the exaltation of the royal prerogative'. This was in contrast to the Whig view that 'the ultimate sovereignty of the people as represented in Parliament was the only true guarantee of the liberty of rights and property of the subject.' Thirdly, there was a general Tory devotion to the Anglican Church as against the Whig plea that freedom of worship should be restored to Protestant dissenters. Their vaunted toleration did not extend to Roman Catholics.

After the Revolution, it has been argued, these were dead issues. The Revolutionary Settlement of 1688 had after all been accepted by the great bulk of the Tories. Nevertheless the Tory attachment to the throne and the Anglican Church separated them in emphasis at any rate from the Whigs with their theoretical commitment to the 'will of the people'. That meant, in the seventeenth and eighteenth centuries, an oligarchy rather than a democracy.

From the beginning of the eighteenth century the determination of the Whigs that at all costs there must be a Protestant, that is a Hanoverian, successor to Anne, while the Tories were, to say the least, divided on this issue, produced a sharp divergence in foreign policy. The Whigs believed that in pursuit of the objective mentioned the French must be defeated with the assistance of the Dutch allies. The Tories, whose rank and file harboured anti-Dutch sentiments, were much less enthusiastic about such a foreign policy and, as will be seen, were ready to make peace with France in a way that was repulsive to the Whigs.

Anne, however, whatever her preference for the Tories, 'shared', in the words of Gila Curtis, 'the view of all her predecessors that she should be perfectly free in making the choice between the Parties, and that the allegiances of her Ministers should be to the Crown and not to any Party or faction.' She worked as a general rule for a government that could occupy the middle position between the party extremes. We are not concerned here with changes among her ministers, except insofar as they affect the House of Lords. She began in fact with a fairly extreme Tory ministry. Gradually she was forced to include a number of Whigs till finally she presided reluctantly over a Whig government. To her unconcealed joy they in turn were overthrown and the Tories were in power for the last few years of her reign. It is not easy for us today to realise that the Tories' strength lay on the whole in the House of Commons, that of the Whigs in the Lords.

One prolonged controversy involving the two Houses arose over the Bill to prevent 'occasional conformity'. At this time the Anglicans had obtained by law a monopoly of public offices. The Dissenters however adopted a tactic of taking Communion in the Established Church which qualified them for the offices in question. They then returned to their own meeting houses and chapels for worship. The Occasional Conformity Bill was intended to put a stop to this stratagem. The High Church Party, in practice the Tories, saw their opportunity with the accession of Queen Anne, a strong supporter of the Established Church.

A Bill was introduced in the Commons late in 1702 and passed quickly despite the opposition of the Whigs. The chief ministers, the Duke of Marlborough and Lord Godolphin, were nominally Tories but they were most anxious not to alienate the Whigs and their Nonconformist supporters, whose support they needed for a successful prosecution of the war. The question was how the defeat of the Bill could be secured in the Lords without infuriating their Tory colleagues. Bishop Burnet reported:

> Both sides took pains to bring up the lords that would vote with them, so that there were above an hundred and thirty lords in the House; the greatest number that had ever been together. The court put their whole strength to carry the Bill.

Prince George, who had received the sacrament as Lord High Admiral, and yet kept his chapel in the Lutheran way, so that he was an occasional communicant, came and voted for the Bill.

The opponents of the Bill added a series of amendments which they knew would be unacceptable to the Commons. There followed several conferences between the two Houses in which each Chamber insisted on its own version of the Bill. The final conference was held on 16 January 1703, in the Painted Chamber. Burnet says that the 'room was the most crowded upon that occasion that had ever been known; so much weight was laid on this matter'.

Following the meeting with the Commons, the Lords returned to their Chamber where they held a series of divisions on each amendment. The vote was close in each instance. In Burnet's words: 'The Lords were so equally divided, that in three questions put on different heads, the *adhering* was carried but by one voice in every one of them; and it was a different person that gave it in all the three divisions.' The Bill could not be proceeded with, but Marlborough and Godolphin and the Whigs realised that the Bill would be brought up again in the following session.

The Queen had certainly done her best for the measure. As the occasional conformist Prince George made his way into the lobby he was reported to have whispered to one of the Whig leaders: 'My heart is vid you'. He may have been relieved at the result. In the next session the Tories carried the Bill through the House of Commons again, though by this time Anne had withdrawn her support.

The Whigs now collected themselves in the Lords for a full scale confrontation. The Bill was read for the first time in the Lords on 14 December 1703. 'After several hours debating, the question was put, whether it would be read a second time and carried in the negative by 12: yeas 59, (17 of them proxies) noes 71 (12 of them proxies); . . . the Prince nor his proxy present.'

The behaviour of Marlborough and Godolphin does not make a favourable impression. They were both present and voted for the Bill, even signing a protest upon its rejection. But they were rightly suspected of being opposed.

The High Church Party were not defeated yet. An attempt was made in the Commons to 'tack the Bill onto the Land Tax' which it was considered that the Lords would not, because it was a money Bill, be entitled to reject. But the managers of the government business redoubled their efforts 'to defeat the tack'. The manoeuvre was defeated in the House of Commons. Marlborough, not presumably much interested in the religious aspect, was overjoyed at the victory of the ministry. He regarded its stability as of major importance to the great coalition against Louis XIV. He wrote to his wife: 'I see the pains that has been taken to carry the tack. If they had succeeded it is what must have disturbed everything, For not only in England but here [he was campaigning in Holland] also they would have been so out of heart, that they would have advanced no monys, so that all our preparations must have stood still. I hope 17 (Nottingham) and 18 (Rochester) did not know these fatal consequences when thay were so earnest for itt for it is most certaine no greater services could be done for France.'

In the long history between the House of Lords and the House of Commons there has been no more palpable example of a victory for the Lords – for good or for ill.

When James VI of Scotland succeeded to the English throne as James I of England in 1603 each country retained its distinct parliament and distinct peerage. For more than a century the English House of Lords was not affected by the union of the two crowns. In 1707, however, the Act of Union was passed between England and Scotland. Now the House of Lords was affected indeed. There were added to the House 16 Lords Temporal, no Lords Spiritual – the established Church of Scotland being Presbyterian and devoid of bishops. For the first time the principle of election was introduced into the constitution of the House of Lords. The 16 Scottish peers were elected by the whole body of Scottish peers not for life, but for each parliament. There were at the time 165 Scottish peers on the Roll. The greater part of them not being also peers of England remained peers without seats in the House of Lords until 1963. In that year an Act was passed which admitted all Scottish peers to the House of Lords and all women with hereditary titles, English or Scottish. At the same time peers were allowed to renounce their titles on succeeding to them.

The Scottish peers were looked upon and felt themselves to be inferior in status to their English colleagues. A letter written somewhat later – by Dundas to Pitt in 1784 – would appear to cover the general relationship from the Union until that time. Dundas forwarded to Pitt the applications of three Dukes and asked him to consider

> what their feelings now are, when by the acquisition of immense independent fortunes enabling them to hold compleat intercourse in society with the peerage of this part of the kingdom, still in point of parliamentary situation the highest in rank in Scotland feel themselves inferior to the lowest of rank of peerage in England.

From the beginning the English peers had been extremely unwelcoming to their new Scottish colleagues. They imposed further limitations on the Scottish peers by rulings of the House of Lords in 1709 and 1711. In 1709 the House of Lords decided that no peer sitting in the House by virtue of a British peerage could vote in peers' elections. While in 1711 the House decreed that no British peerage granted to one who was a peer of Scotland at the time of the Union could entitle that peer to sit in the Upper House. The House would in due course reverse the first decision in 1783 and the second in 1782 (but see below).

The difficulties encountered by the Scots in making their presence felt in the House of Lords are well illustrated by the so-called Hamilton Affair of 1711–1712. Professor Holmes has described it as providing a crisis in Anglo-Scottish relations. He points out that though the Union of Scotland and England came to acquire an air of inevitability, the experiment in the early years came perilously close to failure. There was a storm over the Malt Tax in 1713 when the Union survived hostile opposition from the House of Lords by a mere four votes. Eighteen months earlier the question of the Duke of Hamilton's Patent had produced a similar crisis.

In the Third Parliament of Great Britain, among the 16 representative peers elected by the Scottish nobility on 10 November 1710, was James Douglas, fourth Duke of Hamilton. He had watched several of his fellow countrymen rewarded since the Union. He 'recognised no superior north of the border' (Holmes) and expected for himself a reward which was appropriate to his royal lineage and extensive estates. So he applied for a British dukedom to add to his Scottish titles. The Queen and Harley, now Earl of Oxford and Lord Treasurer, were ready to satisfy what seemed an innocent ambition. However, a tremendous outcry soon broke out. The Whigs were aghast at the idea of adding to the 16 Scottish peers who were regarded, partly because of their poverty, as dependent on the government which had nominated them. They were, it is true, elected, but the Crown influence was considered to be decisive.

The Whigs were determined not to allow further dependent Scots to be ranged against them in a finely-balanced House. They had a shrewd suspicion that if Hamilton's honour was permitted a whole string of new creations all favourable to the Tory Government would much enlarge the Scottish representation in the Lords. The details of the dispute that followed cannot detain us. Finally the Whigs carried the final division by 57 votes to 52. The resolution was carried 'that no Patent of Honour granted to any Peer of Great Britain who was a peer of Scotland at the time of the Union can entitle such peer to sit and vote in Parliament or to sit upon the Trial of peers.' And not even Anne's presence was sufficient, in the event, to deter a number of non-ministerial Tories or even two members of the government itself (Dartmouth and Berkeley of Stratton) from voting with the Opposition.

This decision, reversed, as already mentioned, but not until 1782, was of historic importance for many years. The legal arguments in favour of it were weak. There is no doubt that the anti-Scottish prejudice affected the House of Lords generally as it would have affected any similar body in England at that time. It seems, however, that the so-called election of the Scottish peers had brought a good deal of contempt on the system. Anyone on the official ministerial list seemed certain to be elected. Hamilton does not seem to have done his cause any good by demanding that the Queen should dismiss her Secretary of State, Lord Dartmouth, who had voted against the Patent. He demanded this from the Queen in the name of the whole nation. Dartmouth succumbed. Hamilton proposed that an Act of Parliament might be brought in to confirm his and the Duke of Queensberry's Patents; to which the Queen gave him no answer. The Duke in fact received a snub which seems to have been not unwelcome to the rest of the Scottish peers.

From about 1760 Scotland underwent a powerful renaissance. A new self-confidence translated itself to the Scottish peers, no longer content with their status as second-class citizens. They became more and more eager to integrate themselves more closely into England.

There was a sudden sharp rise in Scottish applications for British peerages. Between 1707 and 1782 few Scots received such honours. Most were unable it seems to support the dignity of a British peerage, but the main cause of the limited number of creations was the Standing Order adopted by the House of Lords in 1711. This was the Order mentioned earlier which prevented any Scottish peer who received a British peerage from taking his seat in the Upper House.

I may be allowed to draw an analogy from my own family history. Our Irish peerage dates from 1756, but my ancestors would not have been entitled to sit in the English parliament until 1821. Under the rule of 1711 he would not have been able to take his seat at that time.

From 1782 when the rule was removed, British peerages with a right to sit in the House of Lords were freely bestowed and much sought after. (In the last decades of the eighteenth century, two distinct national nobilities began to give way to a truly British peerage.) No doubt the motives of the British government in bestowing these peerages were primarily political. But there seems to have been a gradual undermining of the assumptions which underlay the Standing Order of 1711. It ceased to be assumed that 'there should be two distinct peerages of England and that the latter should be subordinate to the former.' (M. McCahill)

One other event of much constitutional interest occurred during the reign of Anne. By 1711 the Tories were back in power. After prolonged negotiations a peace treaty, the Treaty of Utrecht, was signed with France. The Whigs were predictably furious. The most

93

famous piece of literature emerging was Jonathan Swift's pamphlet entitled 'The Conduct of the Allies', which was of immense assistance to the Tories. The prolongation of the war was depicted as a conspiracy among the Allies, connived at by the Whigs.

Anne opened Parliament with a fine statement from the Tory standpoint, much resented by the Whigs. 'I am glad that I can now tell you that notwithstanding the arts of those who delight in war, both time and place are appointed for opening the treaty of a general peace.' Anne was in the habit of disrobing after a formal performance and attending debates in the House of Lords in person, sitting either on the throne or in the colder months on a bench beside the fire (Charles II had done likewise). On this occasion she had to listen to vehement attacks from the Whigs who had incidentally done a deal with some of the extreme Tories. In the course of the debate Lord Anglesey censured the Duke of Marlborough saying that 'the country might have enjoyed the blessings of peace soon after the battle of Ramillies if it had not been deferred by some persons in whose interest it was to prolong the war'. At this Marlborough sprang indignantly to his feet and appealed directly to the embarrassed Queen (who officially was not present) to exonerate him.

The votes were counted. The Government had been defeated by one vote. Its continuance in office seemed precarious. But they had another shot in their locker, though it was one which Anne was very reluctant to use. The Tory leaders persuaded the Queen to create twelve peers to ensure ratification of the Treaty of Utrecht signed in 1713. This use of the prerogative of the Crown to secure a majority for the government in the House of Lords was widely considered to be unprecedented, or at any rate more blatant than anything of the kind that had been done previously. It should be noted that on the accession of George I in 1714 the Whigs created more peers and restored the balance.

This balance in the House of Lords helped to make it 'a golden age'. The reign of George I who succeeded to the throne in 1714 brings home to us the extraordinary ups and downs of the period. Under Queen Anne Robert Harley, Earl of Oxford, had for a long time been the first citizen after the Queen, although she ultimately dismissed him. Soon after George I acceded to the throne and the Whigs had won a general election, Oxford was impeached by the Whig government for his part in the Peace of Utrecht, which had been vehemently opposed by them and the future George I. He languished in prison for two years, but in July 1717 was formally acquitted by the House of Lords of high treason and high crimes and misdemeanours.

The Lords, in notching up another victory against the Commons, were enabled to do so because of a split in the Whig Party. Townsend and Walpole were by this time out of the ministry and were using Oxford's case to embarrass the government's case in the House of Lords. After much to-ing and fro-ing the House of Lords on 24 June 1717 informed the Commons that they must first proceed with the charges of treason. After refusing to meet the Commons in a free conference, they resumed the trial, by this time with the intention of acquitting Oxford. Finally the 107 lords present all solemnly voted to discharge Lord Oxford. He took his seat again in the House of Lords, but the King did not forgive him.

The Earl Stanhope, a leading minister from 1717 to 1721, may be remembered for his moderately successful attempts to cushion the effect of the penal laws on dissenters. He himself, considerably more enlightened in religious matters than most of his contemporaries, would have liked to offer some relief to the Catholics. But in the atmosphere of the time this was a hopeless project. Stanhope is more likely to go down in history for his abortive attempt to create a permanent majority for his ministry in both Houses.

His Peerage Bill of 1719 was designed to prevent any addition to the number of Lords once George had created six new English peers and made some readjustment of the arrangements for Scotland. In future there were to be 25 hereditary Scottish nobles. From then on the monarch's power of making peers was to be restricted to filling vacancies created as lines became extinct. But this measure aroused general indignation, even execration. Walpole in the House of Commons played on the hopes of the back bench MPs of themselves sitting one day in the House of Lords. In December

95

1719 the measure was defeated in the House of Commons by 269 to 177 votes. The House of Commons in my time have never been faced with this kind of decision. As will be seen below, they have, on a crucial occasion in recent years, prevented the rationalisation of the House of Lords. I surmise with confidence they would never have voted for its abolition. Nor would they have voted at any time for a measure such as that of Stanhope.

It should be realised that from 1688 onwards, Parliament had become a far more essential element in the constitutional framework of the country. To quote Sir John Sainty: 'Thereafter annual sessions were inevitable and parliament would no longer be regarded as a more or less temporary institution, to be dispensed with as soon as the financial requirements of the crown had been met.' The new situation, as Sir John has pointed out, imposed on the King's ministers the necessity of reassessing their relationship with Parliament. It became more and more necessary that the Government should have a secure majority in Parliament. This led to important developments in the field of parliamentary management. In each House the role of the Leader became significant.

For much of the eighteenth century we are told that 'little prestige was attached to parliamentary management in the Lords' (Sainty). By September 1780 the concept of a leader 'as opposed to a mere manager' was already in the process of evolution. From 1720 onwards 'the Whiggish hue of the Lords' was in tune with the political climate of the Commons majority. However, the Lords continued to exercise a restraining influence on what might have been the more extravagant excesses of the Commons. As a revising chamber, it was 'far from acting as the king's poodle'. Revolts against the ministry in 1736 over the Quaker Tithes Bill, in 1766 over Rockingham's American policy, and in 1783 over the India Bill, suggest that the Lords still had some political teeth.

INTERLUDE II

The Death of 'The Great Commoner'

The most poignant moment in the long history of the House of Lords must be that of the collapse of William Pitt, Earl of Chatham (1711–1778) on 7 April 1778. He was carried away and died soon afterwards. It is impossible not to use superlatives about Chatham. At the close of the reign of George II, in 1760, Chatham was at the zenith of his glory. 'The Great Commoner', as he was called, 'was the first Englishman of his time, and he had made England the first country in the world.' (Macaulay, Essays, ii. 198). He was the greatest war minister in British history at least until the arrival of Winston Churchill. He was possibly the most powerful orator the House of Commons has ever known – although much less successful in the Lords.

He suffered all his life from gout and, what was worse, a form of nervous depression. There came a time when, though he was the first statesman in the land, he was absolutely incapacitated from all attention to business. From May 1767 to October 1768 he held no intercourse with the outside world. He refused to see his colleagues and even declined to let the King visit him. Who knows what he would have achieved if he had not been so grievously afflicted?

In 1766 he was raised to the peerage with the titles of Viscount Pitt of Burton-Pynsent in the county of Somerset and Earl of Chatham in the county of Kent. No one can ever have so damaged his popularity by accepting a peerage. Lord Chesterfield wrote to his son, 'The joke here is that he has had a fall upstairs and has done himself so much hurt that he will never be able to stand upon his legs again.' His maiden speech in the Lords went quite well but on the next occasion he was held to have flouted the peers. He certainly involved himself in an altercation with the Duke of Richmond. We read in the House of Lords Journal for 10 December 1766, 'Notice

97

was taken of some Words that passed in the Debate between the Duke of Richmond and the Lord Privy Seal: And thereupon the said Lords (being required thereto by the House) severally declared, upon their Honour, "That they would not pursue any further Resentment upon Occasion of the Words that had passed between them".' One assumes that these precautions were being taken to prevent the necessity for a duel. Even 60 years later we find the Duke of Wellington, then Prime Minister, fighting a duel with a fellow peer, though the words used on that occasion had not been uttered in the House.

Chatham's last ten years will be remembered perhaps for all time for his marvellous series of speeches about America. He understood and articulated as no one else could in Britain the feelings of the discontented colonists. His speeches, though there were no established methods of reporting them and it took several weeks to convey them to America, made a lasting impression there.

Perhaps the most famous – until the last one of all – was that delivered on 20 January 1775. He proposed an address to the King requesting him to recall the troops from Boston 'in order to open the ways towards an happy settlement of the dangerous troubles in America'. A few of his phrases must be quoted.

> Indeed I cannot but feel the most anxious sensibility for the situation of General Gage, and the troops under his command . . . their situation is truly unworthy; penned up, pining in inglorious inactivity. They are an army of impotence. You may call them an army of safety and of guard; but they are in truth an army of impotence and contempt; and, to make the folly equal to the disgrace, they are an army of irritation and vexation. . . .

The spirit of liberty which he found in America moved him to his greatest flights of oratory. 'The spirit which now resists your taxation in America, is the same which formerly opposed loans, benevolences, and ship-money, in England: the same spirit which called all England on its legs, and by the Bill of Rights vindicated the English constitution, the same spirit which established the great, fundamental, essential maxim of your liberties, that no subject of

England should be taxed but by his own consent. . . . We shall be forced ultimately to retract. Let us retract while we can, not when we must.' His motion was rejected by 68 votes to 18.

On 30 May 1777, by which time the Americans had declared their independence, he unsuccessfully moved an address to the Crown for the stoppage of hostilities in America. 'You may ravage,' he cried, 'you cannot conquer. It is impossible. You cannot conquer the Americans. I might as well talk of driving them before me with this crutch.' Yet at no time did he ever accept the idea of American independence. His attitude became still firmer when Britain was menaced by the hostility of France and Spain. On 7 April 1778 the Duke of Richmond (his old adversary of 1766 but for a number of years one of his strongest supporters), openly advocated the immediate acknowledgement of American independence. This roused Chatham, by this time in appalling health, to make a final effort.

After Richmond had moved his address, Chatham rose with great difficulty, leaning on his crutches and supported by his son William and Lord Mahon. He spoke, we are told, in a low voice and with frequent pauses yet 'with much animation and decision'. 'I thank God,' he said, 'that I have been enabled to come here this day – to perform my duty. . . . I am old and infirm – have one foot, more than one foot, in the grave – I am risen from my bed, to stand up in the cause of my country – perhaps never again to speak in this House.'

By now the issue had become to him the survival of the British nation. He listed the Government's errors and then demanded, 'Must we on top of all these errors now fall prostrate before the House of Bourbon?' He concluded in heroic fashion, 'My Lords, any state is better than despair. Let us at least make one effort and if we must fall let us fall like men.' The Duke of Richmond replied gently. As he sat down Chatham 'made as if to rise but fell backwards, apparently in a deadly seizure' (Brian Tunstall *William Pitt, Earl of Chatham*).

Lord Townsend we are told ran for water. Strange that there was not a supply of it on the table. 'Everyone was upon his legs in a moment hurrying from one place to another, some sending for assistance, other producing salts and other reviving spirits.'

With the help of his son and Lord Mahon Chatham was lifted into Princes' Chamber and placed on a table, supported with pillows. He received medical attention and was carried to the House of Mr Sergeant Strutt, Clerk to the House of Lords, where he spent the night. Two days later he was taken by coach to Hayes where he died on 11 May. As he lay dying he asked his son William to read the description of the death of Hector from the *Iliad*.

CHAPTER VI

1783–1832

Expansion and Defeat

The modern history of the House of Lords begins in 1783. In the next 20 years the unprecedented creation of peers by William Pitt – the son of Chatham who had supported his father during his final speech – transformed the House. A historian like David Large has picked out the decline of the party of the Crown and the rise of organised parties in the House as a central feature of the period from 1783 to 1837. The majority of officers in the Royal Household, for example, who were peers, tended to become more and more political. By the early 1830s the Government and Opposition alike had a tolerably efficient, if simple, machinery for summoning peers. The Duke of Wellington was assisted by a Whipper-in who did his donkey work whether in office or in opposition. There remained a squeamishness about telling peers how to vote. As one recently-ennobled peer remarked in 1835, 'Who shall make such a request to such august persons as the Dukes of Devonshire and Sutherland?'

As far as I can make out from the other side of the House there is still in the 1980s a reluctance among Conservative peers to admit that the Whip is any kind of directive. They are determined not to be regarded as lobby fodder. Successive Leaders and Chief Whips have liked to dwell on the necessity of using persuasion rather than coercion and on the uncertainty of knowing how many of their nominal supporters would follow their guidance. The Labour peers have not perhaps had time to work out these refinements. We shall find that in the nineteenth century this more professional organisation of the political parties meant in practice an inflexible predominance of the Tories.

The story of the Irish members of the House provides an

illustration of the trend. Under the Act of Union of 1801 28 Irish peers were to be selected by their Irish colleagues to sit in the House of Lords for life (the Scottish peers were elected for a single parliament). The Irish peerage was in fact being continuously reinforced by Pitt's new creations. My own family, who had acquired an Irish peerage in 1756, were not given an English one until 1821 but I have heard Lord Carrington explain how his family progressed during the reign of Pitt. They received an Irish peerage first, not being considered eminent enough for an English one. Only one year later, in 1797, they graduated into what was accepted as a higher form of peerage. Incidentally, the first Lord Carrington was so distraught when his eldest son Robert Smith, MP for Buckingham-shire, supported the Reform Bill that he urged him to avoid his home, 'as I might be tempted to use language which you would never forget. . . .'

To begin with, the Irish representative peerage 'was looked upon simply as a piece of patronage at the disposal of the Government of the day, rather like an extra if inferior rank in the Table of Honours' (David Large). But when the Reform Bill reached the Lords in 1831 the Irish representative peers, who were by this time nearly all Tories, came out against the Ministry. From then onwards the choice of Irish representative peers was virtually made by the leader of the Conservative Party in the Upper House. By this time the number of English peers with Irish economic interests had been much augmented.

I shall be turning in a moment to the great controversial issues of Catholic emancipation and parliamentary reform. But first, I must say a few words about the most dramatic trial before the Lords of the nineteenth century.

The Trial of Queen Caroline

On 5 July 1820 a 'Bill of Pains and Penalties to be inflicted on Queen Caroline' was introduced into the House by the Prime Minister. It was called 'a trial' though it was not a trial in any ordinary sense. The whole story has been told with the utmost skill by Roger Fulford in his book *The Trial of Queen Caroline*. 'A Bill of Pains and Penalties,' wrote Fulford, 'is an Act of Parliament punishing a person without resorting to a legal trial. Such a bill is not a judicial act, though in procedure it may have much in common with a legal trial. As with any other bill it must be passed by sovereign, lords and commons. The machinery is similar to an act of attainder, except that a bill of pains and penalties cannot impose the punishment of death.'

The historian Lecky has described a Bill of Pains and Penalties as 'an extreme, unconstitutional and justly unpopular measure. Liverpool's bill firmly confined the issue to a certain gentleman called Pergami whose relations with the Queen were described as "a most unbecoming and degrading intimacy", "a licentious, disgraceful and adulterous intercourse", "scandalous, disgraceful and vicious conduct". The Bill enacted that "Her Majesty Caroline Amelia Elizabeth shall be deprived of the title of Queen" and that the marriage between her and the King "shall be for ever, wholly dissolved, annulled and made void".'

The excitement, indeed the frenzy, of the general public was unparalleled, though Fulford finds some analogy in the Trial of the Seven Bishops in the reign of King James II. 'While the Queen was in South Audley Street she was the magnet for receiving the mischievous mob every night. After serenading its heroine the mob rioted through the streets smashing windows with indiscriminate glee.' Things had not changed much since the mob demanded the execution of Strafford nearly two centuries earlier, though this time the feeling was overwhelmingly on the side of the defendant.

The arrangements made for the trial, carried through by the Black Rod of the day, are of interest to all students of the House. It was decided that attendance should be compulsory and that absentees should be heavily fined, £100 for the first three days and £50 for each succeeding one. Minors, Roman Catholics, invalids, those out of the country and anyone over 70 was excused from attending. Today, when the average age of active members is said to be 66, a high proportion of these would have been excused. The judges were expected to be present and, though they could not vote, they were expected to advise the House on points of law. Every peer wishing to claim exemption had to write to the Lord Chancellor giving the reason on his honour. The original idea that membership of the Lords involved an obligation to attend was well maintained.

There were at that time on the Roll of the Peerage 367 peers; 260 were expected to attend. 'The House of Lords at that time was a meagre building completely lacking both the size and padded splendour of the present structure: it was not unlike a Chapel without the pews.' (Fulford). It was decided to increase the accommodation for peers by building temporary galleries above the benches normally used by them. A chair and footstool were provided for the Queen immediately within the Bar of the House. 'In this elegant chair the Queen sat through the case in an attitude in which ease and defiance were nicely blended. Sir George Hayter, in his celebrated painting of the scene in the House of Lords, has faithfully recorded the chair, the sitter, the pose.' (Fulford).

The star of the show, apart from the Queen herself, was Henry Brougham, appearing for her. He praised her some years later as 'a Princess of singular accomplishments, quick of apprehension, ready of wit, charitable by instinct and free of all haughtiness and pride, [but] all the time that he was her counsel he referred to her as "that old Bore".' Creevey thought that he absolutely hated her. That was by no means the attitude of the public who cheered her frantically as she made her way to the court and hissed her enemies.

The most violent and famous of all Brougham's interventions came during his cross-examinations of one of the government's witnesses. Brougham suddenly asked who was their client or employer. Working himself up he demanded 'And who is the party? I know nothing about this shrouded, this mysterious being – this retiring phantom – this uncertain shape –

> If shape it might be called that shape has none
> Distinguishable in member, joint, or limb;
> Of substance might be called that shadow seemed,
> For each seemed either. . . .
> What seemed his head
> The likeness of a kingly crown had on.'

Lord Eldon, the Lord Chancellor, had some justification for feeling that he was dealing with an extravagant advocate. George IV is supposed to have said, 'He might at least have left my shape alone.'

The unsavoury impressions created by a wide variety of somewhat disreputable witnesses attracted the censure of the Archbishop of York, the only bishop to vote against the Bill. We can guess what he would have had to say about modern pornography. 'In what way,' he begged to know, 'could the general interests of religion be promoted by the public dissemination through the country, and the introduction into every private family, of those offensive and disgusting particulars with which their lordships had been nauseated throughout this protracted investigation?'

The most surprising intervention came from Lord King, a rather eccentric economist. He asserted that, when the Queen was at Blackheath, she was guilty of indecorum with the Prime Minister, Lord Liverpool (in charge of the Bill) and had played games of Blind Man's Buff with the Chancellor of the Exchequer (Vansittart). 'They never took place,' growled the Prime Minister. Lord King insisted that it had been in the days when 'the noble Earl was looking for means to get into office.' 'Never, I assure you,' said the Prime Minister.

Brougham's peroration was remembered for many decades. It concluded with the words, 'I do here pour forth my own supplications at the Throne of Mercy, that that mercy may be poured down upon the people, in a larger measure than the merits of its rulers may deserve, and that your hearts may be turned to justice.' Lord Erskine rushed from the House in tears. The Lord Chancellor, Lord Eldon, rebuked Brougham sternly: 'Something like a threat was held out to your lordships, that if you passed judgement against the Queen, you would never have the power of passing another judgement. . . . such an address of such a nature, such an address of intimidation, to any court of justice, was never before this hour considered to be consistent with the duty of an advocate. . . .'

The Bill was read a third time. It received a majority of only nine votes. The Government realised that they were beaten and did not pass the Bill to the Commons. The Queen did not benefit in the end. In the following year she beat her hands in vain against the doors of

Westminster Abbey which were closed to her on the occasion of George IV's coronation. A month later she was dead.

Catholic Emancipation

Wellington became Prime Minister at the beginning of 1828. On 24 April he was repeating his firm opposition to Catholic emancipation: 'There is no person,' he said, 'in this House whose feelings are more decided than mine are with regard to the subject of the Roman Catholic claims; and until I see a great change in that quarter, I certainly shall oppose it.'

He himself had not only been brought up in Ireland but he had been Chief Secretary. He considered that he knew the whole question inside out. But by 21 March 1829 he had completely changed his attitude and was giving notice that he would move in the House of Lords the Second Reading of the Roman Catholic Relief Bill which would emancipate Roman Catholics and enable them to sit in the House of Commons and the Lords. Two days later he moved the Second Reading. The election of Daniel O'Connell on 5 July 1828 had proved decisive. Wellington rightly prided himself on knowing when retreat was inevitable.

It was reported that 'The interest excited by the expected discussion on the Roman Catholic Relief Bill collected a great crowd round the doors of their lordships' House at an early hour. Although there was a great number of constables, they could with difficulty keep order. The House was much crowded when the reporters were admitted; the space below the Throne was completely filled, as well as the space allotted to the public. Several ladies were present.' The Duke of Wellington never pretended to what is ordinarily called consistency in politics although his principles remained unchanged. 'The point,' he began, 'which I shall first bring under your Lordships' consideration is the state of Ireland.' The speech was lengthy but that sentence was really the beginning and end of his argument and explanation of why he had apparently changed his views so radically. The speech is best known for one particular passage. 'I am,' he said, 'one of those who have probably passed a longer period of my life engaged in war than most men, and principally, I may say, in civil war; and I must say this – that if I could avoid, by any sacrifice whatever, even one month of civil war in the country to which I am attached, I would sacrifice my life in order to do it.' The contemporary report, unlike Hansard today, informs us that this statement was greeted with cheers.

It is painful to read that the next speaker, the Archbishop of Canterbury, delivered himself of sentiments which today would strike us as shocking.

> Since he had had the honour of a seat in that House, he had uniformly been opposed to granting further concessions to the Roman Catholics. He had always opposed any measure having that object, with pain and diffidence, but never more so than on the present occasion, when he found himself opposed, on this important question, to persons whom he highly respected. But he had a duty to perform which was paramount to all other considerations, – he had a duty to perform to the church to which he belonged, – he had a duty to perform, as a member of the Protestant faith which that church was meant to support, – and he had a duty to perform to the state, which he apprehended might be injured by granting political power to the Roman Catholics.

The Archbishop of Armagh, the Protestant Primate of Ireland, more understandably expressed an equal abhorrence. Support and opposition were expressed by numerous speakers. There were some entertaining passages. 'Lord Kenyon and the Lord Chancellor rose together. The former noble Lord several times attempted to address the House but his voice was drowned in loud and continued cries for the Lord Chancellor. Lord Kenyon said amidst great confusion, "My Lords, I must take the liberty after the imputations which have been passed upon me –"'. Three other noble Lords intervened. 'Finally,' we read, 'Lord Kenyon again rose, and endeavoured to address their lordships, continuing upon his legs, during such loud and general calls for the Lord Chancellor, that not a word that fell from the noble Lord was heard.'

When it came to the vote the score was as follows: Content, present, 147; proxies, 70 – 217. Not Content, present, 79; proxies, 33 – 112. Majority in favour of the Second Reading of the Bill, 105. The Duke of Wellington had triumphed.

The Great Reform Bill

The events of 1831/32 compete with those of 1911 for excitement. In each case an intense conflict was generated between the House of Lords and the government of the day, the latter supported by a large majority in the House of Commons. In each case the Lords ultimately gave way after the country had been carried to the brink. There were, however, obvious differences. In 1831, as contrasted with 1911, there was no question of paying tribute to democratic principles by the main political leaders. No one supposed that by 1832 Lord Grey of the Reform Bill was a democrat. He considered that nobility of birth was superior to nobility of soul.

Before Peel introduced one in the 1830s, the absence of an effective police force made the passions of the London mob much more frightening. In 1831/32 the prospect of revolution was all too present. This could not be said of 1911, although by 1914 the 'Irish Question' led to talk of civil war as being within the bounds of possibility.

'It was inevitable that the great movement for the reform of Parliament which culminated in the Act of 1832 should meet with powerful resistance in the House of Lords – partly because the Chamber in the early decades of the nineteenth century was a citadel of Toryism, partly because so many of its members had a vested interest in the continuance of the exiting system.' So wrote A. S. Turbeville in his impressive essay 'The House of Lords and the Reform Act of 1832'.

As Turbeville points out, the House of Lords had become a citadel of Toryism. During the greater part of the eighteenth century its members had amounted to about 200 persons, predominantly Whig in party complexion. By 1830 it had reached a membership of twice that size and had become predominantly Tory. When Pitt came into office in 1783 there were 238 members of the House; by 1832, 398 members. Turbeville shrinks from assigning precise figures to the various political groups. He points out, however, that by 1832 the House of Lords represented the proper-tied classes with some accuracy. Certainly by this time the peerage had long since come to view the French Revolution with apprehension and abhorrence. Modest reforms suggested in the 1820s were turned down with contempt. A good many members of the Upper House had a vested interest in the continuance of the unreformed House of Commons because of the influence they were able to exert over its composition. Many different estimates have been made of the extent of that control. To mention only one, it was reckoned that 96 peers secured, through influence in the elections, the return of 196 Members of Parliament.

The Whigs had originally seen themselves as favourable to reform but the French Revolution had rendered any serious initiative of that kind an electoral absurdity so long as the war with France continued. Michael Brock in his invaluable book *The Great Reform Act* informs us that 'A few years after Waterloo the political weather began to change. The new generation did not share their elders' alarms. The ideas which had inspired the American and French Revolutions became more familiar and less horrifying to people of property.' As mentioned just now, however, the rather feeble attempts of the Whigs to propose reform in the 1820s got nowhere, despite radical pressures of various kinds which were mounting in the country.

The Catholic Emancipation Act of 1829 had much improved the prospect of reform. It carried the disruption of the Tory Party a stage further and thus weakened and divided the anti-reformers' forces. It brought much encouragement to the radicals who founded, in July 1829, the London Radical Reform Association.

The next event was the General Election which took place in July and August 1830. It does not seem that the balance of parties in the

House of Commons was on paper much affected. But it seems agreed that it brought, in the words of Michael Brock, 'a great access of strength to the reformers'. Wellington and his ministers had expected to emerge with a large majority and been grievously disappointed with the result. Wellington, nevertheless, over-estimated the strength of his position and totally underestimated the public demand for reform. In a debate in the Lords in November 1830, he made what came to be regarded as a calamitous reply to Grey's suggestion that reform was necessary. After paying an extraordinary tribute to the perfection of the British constitution, Wellington concluded, 'Under these circumstances, I am not prepared to bring forward any measure of the description alluded to by the noble Lord. I am not only not prepared to bring forward any measure of this nature but I will at once declare I shall always feel it my duty to resist such measures when proposed by others.' He sat down in a stunned silence. Turning to the Foreign Secretary, Lord Aberdeen, he asked, 'I have not said too much, have I?' Aberdeen warned him lugubriously, 'You'll hear of it.' Outside the Chamber someone asked Aberdeen what the Duke had said. The Foreign Secretary replied hollowly, 'He said we were going out.' And so it proved.

The Whigs after many years in opposition were asked to form a government under Lord Grey. Events moved forward fast. On 1 March of the next year (1831) Lord John Russell introduced the most famous of all the Reform Bills into the House of Commons. But in the still unreformed House of Commons it got bogged down. Grey obtained a dissolution from William IV.

The Lords did their best to sabotage the dissolution. Lord Wharncliffe gave notice of a motion praying the King not to dissolve. From the point of view of the Government it was all-important to persuade the King to prorogue Parliament in person. This was the only way of preventing Wharncliffe's motion being put. The King was anxious to help but there were technical difficulties. It was reported that the tails and manes of the horses required for the royal coach would take five hours to plait. The King is supposed to have assured ministers that if the stage-coach were not ready in time he would go in a hackney-coach. In the event, this was not necessary, but the proceedings in the Lords until his arrival were possibly the most disorderly in the history of the Chamber. Lord Londonderry, for example, had to be held back by four or five peers from offering his opponents violence. Brougham, the Lord Chancellor, was subjected to prolonged hooting but continued to speak until he heard the guns announcing the arrival of the King. The King, having put the crown on his head, though there had been no coronation, entered the Chamber in time to cut short a speech of vicious eloquence from the Tory Earl of Mansfield. He duly prorogued the House.

A friend told the diarist Greville:

> that in his life he never saw such a scene; and as he looked at the king upon the throne with the crown loose upon his head, and the tall, grim figure of Lord Grey close beside him, with the sword of state in his hand, it was as if the king had got his executioner by his side; and the whole picture looked strikingly typical of his and our future destinies.

The Reformers swept home to a tremendous election victory, and the Tories were utterly routed. The Bill was re-introduced and carried through the House of Commons, but voted down by a majority of 41 in the Lords. One is sorry to read that 21 out of 23 bishops opposed the Bill (they were to redeem themselves in 1911). The Bill was brought in again and again defeated in the Lords. Grey demanded the creation of at least 50 peers. The King refused any kind of mass creation. Grey then resigned.

The King now commissioned the Duke of Wellington to form a government, informing him, however, that he must bring in the extensive measure of reform to which the country was now entitled (though the King's dislike of reform was almost as intense as that of Wellington). Wellington's task was rapidly seen to be impossible. In spite of his initial reply, 'I am perfectly ready to do what His Majesty may command me', revolutionary arrangements were being made for barricading Birmingham, Manchester and other cities. His prospective Chancellor of the Exchequer, Alexander Baring, was howled down in the House of Commons. Wellington was compelled to inform the King that he could neither form a government nor find support in the Commons. Grey told the King that he must either promise to create a sufficient number of peers, or face the possibility of insurrection. This time the King gave way and agreed to Grey's request. The Duke of Wellington promised to abstain from further opposition to the Bill and make his friends do likewise, but he certainly beat a fighting retreat.

Lord Holland, a member of his Cabinet, left behind a fascinating diary. He describes the strong language used by Wellington against the Bill in the Lords. He announced, 'The man who threatens was as criminal as the man who should create Peers.' Every sentence, according to Holland, 'breathes enmity to the principles, details and authors of the Bill'.

On a later date Holland recorded 'Nothing could exceed the violence and acrimony of the invective of the Lords in all the debates before going into Committee and occasionally in the Committee itself.' But their teeth had been drawn. On 4 June 1832 Grey moved that the Fourth Reform Bill be now read a third time. The agreement of the Duke of Wellington not to oppose the measure any further and to advise his friends in that sense had taken most of the steam out of this long-running conflict. In the event the Contents were 106, Not Contents 22. The vast majority of the peers abstained. There were little touches in the debate which will bear reproducing: 'The Earl of Harrowby rose and said that he remembered, a good many years ago, to have heard a story told of a Member of the Irish Parliament, who, after putting several questions to the members of the Government without obtaining any reply, addressed himself to the Speaker and said (if the record were correct), "Mr. Speaker, are we in the Irish Parliament, or in a Turkish Divan? Are we to be strangled by mutes?"' He [Harrowby] referred to the degradation to which the Government had reduced the House. He finished by expressing himself grievously disappointed by the conduct of the noble Earl. Earl Grey, in replying, informed the House that in his state of health he was afraid his indisposition would be apparent to their Lordships before he sat down. He had hoped that he would have been spared the pain to himself and the trouble to their Lordships of addressing them at all. He then proceeded to refute the attack on his own honour and that of his colleagues at considerable length. We are told however that: 'The noble Earl terminated his speech abruptly in consequence of the indisposition of which he had complained at the beginning.' Fortunately the result was a foregone conclusion.

The Bill passed into law. The Lords had challenged it and, indeed, after the election seemed ready to challenge the electorate itself. Through the firmness of Grey, the reluctant compliance of the King and in the last resort, Wellington's sense of the realities of the situation, they had given way.

CHAPTER VII

1832–1905

The Tories in Control

The extravagant hopes and fears attached to the Reform Bill of 1832 were equally disappointed. The Lords lost some of their control through patronage of the House of Commons but this decline took a good many years to come about.

Macaulay wrote gleefully in 1833, 'Nobody seems to care one straw for what the Peers may say about any public matter. A Resolution of the Court of Common Counsel, or of a meeting at Freemasons' Hall, has often made a greater sensation than this declaration of a branch of the Legislature against the Executive Government. The institution of the Peerage is evidently dying a natural death.'

But events proved him hopelessly wrong. To start with, the aristocracy continued to be represented in the House of Commons in large numbers for a long time to come. In 1865 it was calculated that a quarter of the members of the House of Commons were connected with 31 great families. The Whigs as a Party had no desire to impair an estate of the realm. The Tories, led by Wellington, had just as little a desire to provoke a revolution.

The country gradually moved in a conservative direction. The Whigs lost ground in the Election of 1835 and still more in that of 1837. The Tories returned in strength in 1841. Some English legislation of permanent value was passed in the early 1830s but the attitude of the House of Lords to Ireland in these years was easily predictable. By the time the first reformed Parliament was opened on 29 January 1833, the Irish interest in the Lords had become a formidable body. Virtually one peer out of every four had a stake in Ireland through the ownership of land, and the majority of these were men whose economic interests were exclusively centred on their Irish estates. 'In the event the legislation affecting Ireland between 1833 and 1841 was almost as much the work of Peel and Wellington as of the Ministers concerned.' (David Large). Wellington, in fact, had a very difficult hand to play. Himself a strong instinctive Tory, he retained his fear of possible revolution if the ultra-Tory extremists got out of hand.

The Tory ascendancy during the early part of the nineteenth century is well known. What is not so familiar is that when the Peelites seceded from the Conservative Party and gradually moved into alliance with the Whigs, the Tories were for a short time almost balanced by a combination of Whigs and Peelites.

This did not last long. The inherent tendencies of an hereditary House to move in a conservative direction soon asserted itself. In 1860 there was a majority of 89 against the Second Reading of Gladstone's Paper Duty Bill. Gladstone himself and the Liberal Party generally became steadily more radical and simultaneously Liberal strength in the Lords rapidly declined.

Walter Bagehot, in his *English Constitution* (1867 revised 1872) treated the House of Lords as belonging to the dignified rather than the efficient part of the constitution. He quoted the letter written by the Duke of Wellington to Lord Stanley (later fourteenth Earl of Derby and Prime Minister), relating how he persuaded hostile peers to stay away from the House of Lords so that the Reform Bill could become law, and had afterwards worked to lessen conflict between his House and the reformed House of Commons. He had guided the peers to what Bagehot considered their true position. In this way the House of Lords had effectively become a Chamber with (in most cases) a veto of delay and (in most cases) a power of revision, but with no other rights or powers. Already, however, this way of looking at things was beginning to seem out of date.

When the Liberals came back in 1869 the Irish Church Bill much disliked by the great majority of the Lords obtained a Second Reading. The other measures of the government had, however, a rough time. The Bill to abolish the purchase of army commissions was rejected by the Lords, but the government found a way of achieving its purpose without legislation. The Ballot Bill twice failed in the Upper House. It needed all Disraeli's skill to get it through at the third attempt.

Disraeli was in power from 1874–1880. When Gladstone came back, the House of Lords was soon at work seriously amending the Irish Land Bill of 1881 and the amending Arrears Bill of 1882. On these occasions they gave way eventually. But the Reform Bill of 1884 produced a major collision. In the Lords a basic amendment was carried against the Government by 205 to 146. At this point the Liberal or Radical leaders began to let themselves go. Joseph Chamberlain, still at this stage a radical, referred to the peers as 'the representatives of a class who toil not, neither do they spin'. John Morley announced that the House must be either 'ended or mended'. All this was just over a 100 years ago.

The Liberals had for a long time remained very strong on the top level. Gladstone's Cabinet in 1880 contained only twelve members, but of these one was a duke, one a marquis and five were earls, in other words a majority were peers. Yet still the defections went on and became a flood when Gladstone came out for Home Rule in 1886. This, in Rosebery's words, 'threw the great mass of Liberal peers into the arms of the Conservative majority.' Meanwhile there was a potent new intellectual influence on the Conservative side.

It is impossible to divorce the drastic change in the House of Lords' attitude during the last quarter of the century from the personality of Lord Salisbury. Apart from his other claims to fame, he was Prime Minister for a short time in 1885, then for six years from 1886 to 1892 and again from 1895 to 1902.

Salisbury's deeply considered attitude to the House of Lords was well expressed when he was urging the rejection of the 1872 Ballot Bill. 'I am rejecting the Bill on the second reading for this reason. It appears to me of vital necessity that our acceptance of bills to which we *are opposed should be regulated on some principle.* If we listen to the Liberals we should accept all important bills which had passed the House of Commons by a large majority. But that in effect would be to efface the House of Lords. Another principle – which is, so far as I can gather, what commends itself to Derby [the fifteenth Earl] – is to watch newspapers, public meetings and so forth, and only to reject when "public opinion" thus ascertained, growls very loud. This plan gives a premium to bluster and will bring the House into contempt. The plan which I prefer is frankly to acknowledge that the nation is our master, though the House of Commons is not, and to yield to our own opinion only when the judgement of the nation has been challenged at the polls and decidedly expressed.' More than a century has passed since Salisbury uttered those influential words. I know well that they are echoed by many thoughtful conservative peers in the 1980s.

This book, as stated earlier, is a history of the House of Lords not of the aristocracy. I cannot, however, ignore the learned work of Professor Lawrence Stone on the latter subject. He has insisted that the date of 1880 marked 'a major turning point' in the political authority of the landed élite for three hundred and forty years previously. According to Stone 'the élite had maintained a highly stable, social and political system'. 'But now,' says the Professor, 'their time was up. The political and economic debacle between 1880 and 1925 was of lasting importance.' I will not attempt to challenge Professor Stone on his social and economic analysis, as that task has been undertaken by others. It will be noticed, however, that the alleged political debacle took an odd form if we adopt 1880 as a starting point. It seems to be generally accepted that the aggressiveness and the authority of the Lords increased from then on. At any rate until they came to grief in 1911.

In one of the corridors of the House today there is a picture of a debate in the House of Lords on Gladstone's second Irish Home Rule Bill in 1893. It had passed the House of Commons (of course with the help of the Irish vote) but was defeated in the Lords by 419 votes to 41. An extraordinarily large vote considering that there were about 600 members of the House at that time. It has, I think, only once been exceeded in recent years although the House today is on paper almost twice as large. My father and one of my grandfathers were in the huge majority! The House of Lords had reached the position when an hereditary peerage could snap its fingers at the government.

Gladstone would have liked to dissolve Parliament in the face of this appalling situation but his colleagues declined. Rosebery, the new Prime Minister, was soon writing to the Queen: 'When the

117

Conservative Party is in power, there is practically no House of Lords, but the moment a Liberal government is formed, this harmless body assumes an active life and its activity is entirely exercised in opposition to the government.' Some months later he reported: 'Nearly if not quite half of the Cabinet is in favour of a single Chamber. The more prominent people in the Liberal Party appear to be of the same opinion.' But the Liberal leaders did little more than flap their hands. The Tories triumphed at the General Election of 1895 and again in 1900. They were in power for ten years and naturally had no trouble with the House of Lords during that time.

The Debate on the Home Rule Bill of 1893

No debate could be more instructive. In the first place it throws a blazing light on the attitude of the House of Lords of that day towards Ireland. In the second place it is just as revealing of their attitude towards their own position. The Bill was introduced a year after a General Election. The Liberal Party had returned to power but were dependent on the Irish members for a majority in the House of Commons. The sincerity of their attachment to Home Rule was highly dubious in the eyes of their opponents. The Bill was introduced into the House of Lords by Earl Spencer, at that time First Lord of the Admiralty. In some respects he had a strong position in the Lords. Much respected personally, he was looked on as having been a firm Lord Lieutenant who had shown no undue softness towards trouble-makers. On the other hand his conversion to Home Rule was still comparatively recent. It was widely attributed to his personal loyalty to Mr Gladstone. 'An old man in a hurry,' was one of the more kindly phrases applied to the latter. See page 25 above for Lord Hailsham's use of the quotation.

Spencer began his speech with a long historical disquisition which makes good reading today. His message, however, boiled down to the impossibility of securing the loyalty of Ireland and therefore law and order unless some measure of Home Rule was extended. He would have known while he was speaking that the Bill would be overwhelmingly defeated. With the understatement then and now characteristic of the House of Lords he observed: 'I know that I shall probably not get the assent of the noble Lords opposite or behind me to what I am now going to say, but if the Bill does what we expect it will bring contentment to the Irish people.' Hansard records at this point: 'Opposition laughter and ironical cheers'. The gallant Lord Spencer continued: 'I am quite aware of the feeling which that cheer indicates but I am bound to state what I honestly believe.' He struggled on desperately: 'I am aware,' he said, 'that the people of Ulster view this Bill with great dislike and oppose it most vigorously. It has been said [by Randolph Churchill] that Ulster will fight and Ulster will be right . . . in my opinion the fears of Ulster are quite groundless . . . knowing the generosity of the people of Ireland I cannot but think that these appalling prognostications will come to nothing and that when Parliament has decided to pass a Home Rule measure the men of Ulster will come forward willingly and take part in the government of their Ireland.' He insisted that no one was a stronger opponent of separation than he was but contended that under this Bill separation would be impossible. No one of course can say whether separation to the extent it has been taken since would have taken place if the Home Rule Bill had been carried. No one can say whether the Six Counties would, today, be governed as a separate community from the 26. For my part I am quite sure that the United Kingdom in the form that it was being defended by the Unionists of that day would have disappeared in any case. I am equally sure that the main results could have been secured without violence.

The first speaker for the Opposition was the Duke of Devonshire. As Lord Hartington he had been a leading Whig and, on one occasion at least, had had the chance of becoming Prime Minister. He possessed a beautiful home in Ireland in addition to all his English property. His brother Lord Frederick Cavendish had been murdered in the Phoenix Park, Dublin, with surgical knives soon after becoming Chief Secretary for Ireland. Various stories were told of Hartington to suggest that he was not particularly bright. He was always supposed to have said, 'I dreamt that I was speaking in the House of Lords and woke up and found I was,' but in fact he was a keen-witted statesman. There was nothing drowsy about his speech on the present occasion. Like Joseph Chamberlain he had left Gladstone and the Liberal Party on this very issue of Home Rule. He was, by this time, as indeed was Lord Salisbury who would be speaking later, a committed foe of the aspirations of the Irish people.

For our purposes what he had to say about the rights and duties of the House of Lords is more significant than his views on Ireland. He admitted that there were certain limits to the powers of the Lords: 'You know that not being a Representative Assembly, and not backed by the strength which a representative character gives to a Legislative Body, and not sharing altogether the democratic principles which are making progress in this as in other countries, it would be unwise, impolitic, and unpatriotic to insist upon your personal political convictions by enforcing them in opposition to what is believed to be the decided view of the country.'

He pointed to the case of the Reform Bill of 1832 and 'of later Reform Bills'. The Lords had given way because they were satisfied that the will of the British people favoured the proposed measures. But he entirely refused to admit that that was the situation here. 'It has been absolutely impossible,' he said, 'to form any opinion as to what the real desire and wish of the people is upon this most vital question. We contend that it is a question large enough to justify us in refusing to pass this measure into law until that question is settled beyond a shadow of a doubt.' He would not even admit that it had 'indirectly that approval through the representatives of the people in Parliament, that is, the House of Commons'. Once again we meet the doctrine which we have encountered in the writings of Lord Salisbury before and after he succeeded to the title. His hostility to the Bill was total. It was summed up in his peroration: 'We hope that the people will support us to abide by the union of the United Kingdom which we believe was decreed by nature and to which laws and treaties have only given a written sanction and record.' There could be no arguing with that primitive faith. He was not likely to convince anybody who did not share it but in the House of Lords that evening it would have been shared by most of his audience.

The second Government speaker was the Earl of Rosebery, generally considered at this time to be the most felicitous orator of the day. He did not fail to live up to that reputation. He twice quoted poetry and indulged in many happy flights of fancy comparing the course pursued by the Opposition in the House of Commons to the performers in a bullfight. He developed that theme at some length. One joke comes through on the printed page: 'The noble Lord, Lord Muskerry, who speaks with great vehemence, told us two or three times in the course of his speech that he knew all about Ireland. That is not the question. The question on this occasion is – I do not wish to put it offensively [the formula still used today] – what does Ireland know about him?' He suggested Ireland knew nothing about him whatsoever. One hopes he extracted a laugh even from the ranks of Tuscany.

But as an advocate for Home Rule he was, to say the least, half-hearted. 'I speak,' he said, 'as a witness but not an enthusiastic witness in favour of Home Rule'. He wasn't likely to wring much support with that admission nor with this one. 'You may be certain,' he said, 'in regard to this controversy, of the infallibility of the course you have pursued or have proposed to pursue. I may frankly say that they are by no means sure of mine. I am not certain about anything with regard to Ireland.' (Opposition cheers.)

He rather weakly commented that he 'was never more gratified than by those cheers'. He was to become known as 'the orator of Empire' and he was already regarded correctly as a Liberal Imperialist. 'It is,' he said, 'because I want to avert a practical dismemberment of the Empire that I stand before your Lordships as a supporter of Home Rule tonight.' He did his best but his heart was obviously not in the job.

That criticism could not be levelled at Lord Salisbury who made the final Opposition speech. He did not attempt to say anything of importance about the relations between the Houses. He expressed what seems now an extraordinary animosity towards the Irish people. He laid a good deal of stress on strategic questions but the Earl of Kimberley who wound up for the Government and seems to the present writer to have put his finger on the strength or weakness (according as one looks at it) of the Unionist case. He told the vast Unionist majority that their arguments were merely 'the means by which you veil your ineradicable distrust of the Irish'.

That might have seemed a rather crude assumption but there was much to justify it in Lord Salisbury's diatribe about them. 'When the era of religious conflict arrived it was not true that the differences were caused by religion, but their views on religion lent themselves to the native, constant, incurable differences and quarrelsomeness of the race' and a good deal more to the same effect. Family attitudes change even where family traditions are powerful. From personal experience I know what a high regard Mr de Valera, then Prime Minister of Ireland, came to hold for Lord Salisbury's grandson, then Dominion Secretary, during a period of extreme delicacy in British/Irish relations. *That* Lord Salisbury told me how touched he had been by Mr de Valera's kindness when he lost one of his sons. His grandfather was a great man. It is almost incredible that he should have entertained the views that he held about the Irish.

As already mentioned when it came to the vote the Bill passed by the Commons was thrown out by 419 votes to 41. The picture in the corridor immortalises the scene and surely conveys an awful warning.

INTERLUDE III

Some Other Aspects of the Nineteenth Century
Noble Families Again

We must turn aside to ask how the Houses of Stanley, Russell and Cecil were faring.

The fourteenth Earl of Derby was born in 1799 and succeeded to the title in 1851. During the preceding 20 years he had been very prominent and, it may be said, mobile politically. He started as a Whig then briefly became a Canningite Tory, then a Whig again, then a Tory, finishing as a Tory Prime Minister for three short periods. In Grey's Whig government of 1830, he was Chief Secretary for Ireland, helping the government considerably in the struggle to steer the 1832 Reform Bill through the Commons. He was no enthusiast for parliamentary reform; he insisted that the vote should be confined to responsible citizens who had a reasonable financial stake in the country. He persuaded himself that the Bill would not impair the influence of the aristocracy.

In 1833 he was promoted to the office of Secretary for War and the Colonies, but resigned when a commission was set up to inquire into the revenues of the Church of Ireland and to assess what percentage should be diverted to social welfare.

By the time Peel formed his Government in 1841 Stanley was a leading Tory and was re-appointed Secretary for War and the Colonies. Later he three times presided over minority Conservative governments, 1852–57, 1858–59, 1866–68. He was technically responsible during this last period for the famous Reform Bill of 1867 which conferred the vote on the working men of the towns. But the main credit must go to Disraeli, Derby by this time being a very sick man.

The fourteenth Earl was a fine classical scholar and known as the Rupert of Debate. His son, the fifteenth Earl (1826–1893), resembled his father in his classical abilities, winning a first class degree in that subject at Cambridge. He seems to have been just as flexible but distinctly more liberal. Later Sir Charles Dilke was to say of him: 'My low opinion of Lord Derby as a politician does not prevent my thinking that in private he is a most agreeable man.' This Lord Derby was made Colonial Secretary in his father's second ministry (1858–59) and Foreign Secretary in his third. His liberal tendencies brought him trouble with his party when he declined to vote against the Irish Land Bill of 1870. He took much interest in such matters as sanitary reform and technical education.

In 1878 we find him Foreign Secretary again, resigning office because of the bellicosity which the Prime Minister, Disraeli, was showing towards Russia. Resembling his father in the rapidity of his movement from one party to another he became Colonial Secretary in Mr Gladstone's second administration (1882). But he had not finished his transmigrations. Gladstone's Home Rule Bill was too much for him and he finished as a Liberal Unionist.

The fourth Duke of Bedford (1710–1771) is not to be confused with the fourth Earl, who succeeded to his title in 1732. When Bedford entered politics, Sir Robert Walpole and his faction among the Whigs had long been in power. Bedford however was very disenchanted by what seemed to him the corrupt methods of the Whig government. He soon emerged as a leading opponent of Walpole and with his exalted rank and far-reaching estates, he was readily accepted as a recognised leader of the Whigs. His career need not be followed in detail here. It is claimed on his behalf that he was a very successful Lord Lieutenant of Ireland. Wiffen says of him that: 'Few personages during their lives were subjected to more indiscriminate abuse from the organs of those parties who were at variance with him than he.'

Since then the Dukes of Bedford have not been prominent in public life, though the last duke but one aroused a good deal of odium in the House of Lords by his pacifist views. I myself have a recollection of one occasion when the traditional courtesy of the House towards an eccentric faltered. There have been, however, many members of the collateral branches of the family which have won much admiration, sometimes along with painful antagonism nevertheless.

One must at least mention Lord John Russell, first Earl Russell (1792–1878), twice Prime Minister, and his grandson, Bertrand Russell, FRS (1872–1970), arguably the best-known philosopher of the present century, a sworn enemy of the Christian religion, a master of English prose and a man who twice went to prison for his beliefs.

Lord John Russell, as he will always be thought of, spent three years at Edinburgh University. In 1813, aged 21, he was returned for the ducal borough Tavistock, but he was rebellious from the first. He opposed the repressive measures of 1817. He protested that the causes of the discontent at home could be removed by remedial legislation. On this issue he resigned his seat in 1817 and was with difficulty persuaded a year later to return to Parliament, this time representing a family borough in Devon. Soon he was beginning his long advocacy of parliamentary reform, paying at one point the penalty for his support for Catholic emancipation by temporary absence from Parliament.

In 1828 he carried a motion for inquiry into the Test Acts and must be credited with a large share of responsibility for its repeal soon afterwards. And so it went on, with John Russell at all times the fearless champion of reform. It fell to his lot as Paymaster-General (though without a seat in the Cabinet), to introduce the Great Reform Bill into the House of Commons. The Whig ministry, as we have seen, was soon defeated, but after the General Election returned with increased strength. When the Reform Bill became law in June 1832, by a sure instinct the public regarded Lord John Russell, not the weaker Earl Grey, as its champion.

We must pass over Russell's career till the resignation of Peel in 1846. It should be mentioned however that in Melbourne's new administration of 1835, he became Home Secretary and Leader of the House of Commons, and later Secretary of State for the Colonies. The Whigs were crushingly defeated in the General Election of 1841, Russell however winning a personal triumph.

In 1845 he committed himself to the reform of the Corn Laws. When Peel was forced to resign on this issue and the Tory Party were gravely split, it was natural that Russell should become Prime Minister, a post he held from 1846 to February 1852.

In November 1850, he issued a public letter denouncing the threatened assumption of ecclesiastical titles by the Roman Catholic bishops, another manifestation of the lingering anti-popery of his family. He ejected Palmerston, his Foreign Secretary, from his post after his unauthorised recognition of the French coup d'etat of 1851, only to be ejected in his turn by Palmerston taking his revenge. In due course he led the Lower House again for some time as Foreign Secretary. At the Vienna Conference (1855) he was England's representative and immediately afterwards became Secretary of the Colonies, but he was held to have made mistakes at Vienna and was forced to retire soon afterwards.

He has been described as being for some years after this 'the stormy petrel of politics', but it was not long before he was back in high office – Foreign Secretary in Palmerston's 1860 ministry and Prime Minister for a short while after Palmerston's death. He is notably remembered for his restraining influence on British politics during the American civil war and his warm espousal of the unification of Italy. He retired after failing to carry a further Reform Bill, a cause to which he had always been faithful. Articulate to the last he died on 28 May 1878, nearly 86 years old.

His grandson Bertrand Russell, born six years earlier, was made a Ward of Court in protest at his father's desire to have him brought up an agnostic. He was brought up by his grandmother, Lord John Russell's widow. Instead of being sent to school he was taught by governesses and tutors, acquiring a perfect knowledge of French and German. In his adolescence he shook off the stern Protestant influences of his grandmother, and his father's desire that he should become an agnostic was more than fulfilled. He was determined that the family title should continue. His second wife, Dora, has told us how reluctant she was to be married when a child was on the way. The son in question, who died in 1987, was a friend of mine in the House of Lords. His mother once described him to me as the most unaggressive man she knew. It takes all sorts to make a Russell. The present Earl though barely middle aged, is already a distinguished historian.

One of the most popular members of the House of Lords at the present time is the fourth Lord Ampthill. He handles the catering arrangements with exceptional skill and on that and other grounds is a most valued member of the House. But he had hard work getting here. His father died in 1973, but it was only after three years of argument before the Home Secretary, Attorney General and finally the Committee for Privileges, at a cost of tens of thousands of pounds, upheld his right to take his seat. His father, after being divorced by his mother, had had another son by his third wife who claimed the title on the grounds that Geoffrey Russell, now Lord Ampthill, was illegitimate. I need not set out the arguments presented on both sides by learned counsel, except to say that all four legal members of the Committee for Privileges (law lords) had no doubt whatever about the legitimacy of Geoffrey Russell and the five lay Lords concurred. What is interesting for our purpose is the composition of the Committee for Privileges, four law lords and five lay members of the House. No one who knows the lay members would suppose that they would be content to act as cyphers. In fact they intervened strenuously in questions to Counsel. Lord Ampthill had the disagreeable experience of listening for four days to arguments at once technical and heated as to whether he was or was not legitimate. Mercifully it turned out all right in the end, and the Queen was given the correct advice.

'For more than a century and a half,' wrote Lady Gwendolen Cecil of her forebears, 'the general mediocrity of intelligence which the family displayed was varied by instances of quite exceptional stupidity.' Kenneth Rose says of James, the fourth Earl (1666–1694), that although barely 28 when he died 'he achieved much fame, all of it undesirable'. This seems a little harsh. He gambled away £40,000 and hardly lived on his means, but there is no reason to assume that he was insincere when he became a Catholic. It was admittedly unfortunate that he took this step two or three months before the Catholic James II was chased out of the country. One can surely sympathise with him in his famous cry, 'Oh, God, I turned too soon.' But by present day standards it was iniquitous that he should be incarcerated in the Tower. It was surely to his credit that on his release he stuck to his new faith and continued to stand up for his former king.

In order to make sure that his sons William and Charles should be brought up under Catholic influences he sent them to live in Paris. There they shared the same bed, and it could not have been foreseen that in a duel to the death, William would be slain by Charles. James, the seventh Earl, in retrospect represents the beginning of a revival. The parliamentary influence he put at the disposal of Pitt was considerable. He was created a Marquis in 1789 and a Knight of the Garter in 1792. Incidentally, Kenneth Rose calls our attention to the fact that the Salisbury Cecils have acquired eight Garters to which will be added four more from the Exeter line. Can any other family rival this?

The second Marquis, James (1791–1868), evoked in Kenneth Rose's happy phrase 'a similar indifference from his contemporaries'. Like his father, he became a member of the Privy Council, and achieved the Garter. He attained Cabinet office briefly in two Conservative governments, hence his portrait in the Leaders' Room in the House of Lords. He is usually remembered, however, for his marriage to the 'Gascoigne heiress' who is credited with introducing the red blood which the Cecils by that time appeared to be badly in need of. Whatever the explanation, the next Marquis, Robert Cecil (1830–1903) was in a different category of distinction from that of any of his predecessors since Robert Cecil died in 1612.

I have discussed at some length the profound influence exerted by the doctrine of Robert Cecil, who succeeded to the title in 1868, on the thinking and the actions of Conservative peers in the late nineteenth and the early twentieth centuries. Indeed I would believe that they still dominated the outlook of Bobbity Salisbury, his grandson, in the years after the Second World War. Here I need only mention that he was a Conservative MP for Stamford from 1863 to 1868, Secretary of State for India 1866–67 and 1874–78, Secretary of State for Foreign Affairs 1878–80, and Prime Minister from June 1885 to January 1886, from 1886 to August 1892, and

June 1895 to July 1902. Till near the end he continued, while Prime Minister, to hold the position of Foreign Secretary.

Three of his sons, the eldest, 'Jim', and two others, Robert and Hugh, became leading politicians, though Hugh, an eccentric of much brilliance, never held office. Robert's name will always be connected with the League of Nations. No other Englishman contributed half as much to that noble conception. David Cecil insists that 'the life story of his [Salisbury's] children shows the magnetic strength of my grandfather's personality. In spite of the fact that they were so vital and so diverse and that he made a conscious effort not to impose his point of view on them, they grew up wholly and lastingly committed to it; and especially in regard to what they thought the two most important subjects in life, religion and politics.' In this rapid survey, I will concentrate on only one of the family, the fourth Marquis, 'Jim Salisbury', whom I was able to observe at close quarters during my first two years in the House of Lords. He lacked the mental brilliance possessed by his father, at least one of his brothers, and his son Lord David, but I am ready to accept him as being as saintly as any politician is likely to be. David Cecil, his son, gives a touching account of his self-abnegation. Kenneth Rose describes the total disregard of self with which he showed goodwill towards the Oxford Group who were by no means generous to him. The fact remains that on all the main political issues, he was quite exceptionally reactionary, whether it was the House of Lords, Ireland, or India. One does not have to be exceptionally left-wing to feel that there was some contradiction here.

Perhaps two sentences in David Cecil's account give us something of a clue . . . 'He looked on his privileged position as a trust only to be justified by a life given up to work for the good of others.' He certainly lived up to that ideal of personal conduct. But with that thought should go this one: 'He was a leader of a die-hard resistance to the Parliament Act of 1911 which broke the power of the House of Lords. To accept it, thought my father, would be to abdicate his inherited responsibilities.' In other words, he had inherited a profound sense of obligation to defend the interests, not of himself for whom he cared nothing, but of his social class and the kind of Britain that he loved so deeply.

David Cecil and Kenneth Rose both reluctantly conclude that the Cecils did not exert the influence which should have flowed from their lofty position and outstanding gifts of mind and character. Both authors recognise that the Cecils were associated with losing causes. Why they remained loyal to those causes is a matter for speculation. I would suggest that outside religion, love of family governed all their attitudes.

The Judicature of the House of Lords since 1800

The piece of legislation passed during the nineteenth century which had most obvious impact on the House of Lords was the Appellate Jurisdiction Act of 1876. In the time of the great jurist Sir William Blackstone (1723–1780) it was said that in the law reposed 'an entire confidence in the honour and conscience of the noble persons who compose this important assembly, that they will make themselves masters of those questions upon which they undertake to decide, since upon their decision all property must finally depend.' But by 1876 the time had gone by when it was thought that legally unqualified persons were capable of performing judicial functions. From then on the House of Lords in its judicial capacity was an entirely professional body connected only by a narrow thread to what the general public referred to as the House of Lords.

Under the provisions of the Appellate Jurisdiction Act of 1876 no appeal could be heard and determined in the House of Lords except in the presence of three at least of the following persons, all of whom bear the general name of Lords of Appeal: the Lord Chancellor of Great Britain, for the time being, peers who have previously held his office; peers who hold or have previously held the office of Lord Chancellor of Ireland; paid judges of the Judicial Committee of the Privy Council; judges of one of Her Majesty's Superior Courts of Great Britain or Ireland; and 'the Lords of Appeal in Ordinary'.

The Act enabled the Sovereign to create four Lords of Appeal in

Ordinary, enjoying the rank of Baron for life, and since 1887 entitled for life to sit and vote in the House. The maximum permitted number of Lords of Appeal was increased to six in 1913, seven in 1929, nine in 1947 and eleven in 1968. Strengthened in this fashion, the House of Lords has remained the highest Court of Appeal for all except Scottish criminal cases.

The steps by which this came about are traced in detail by Robert Stevens in his massive work *Law and Politics – the House of Lords as a Judicial Body* (1979). At the end of the eighteenth century the peers still attached much importance to the retention of their judicial function. From their own point of view the most important aspect of the Lords' work was its original jurisdiction. Impeachment, however, a favourite with the lay peers, provided opportunity for intrigue and a rather sadistic public spectacle. In this spectacle many peers participated actively.

At the end of the eighteenth century the impeachment of Warren Hastings occupied no less than 148 days spread over more than seven years (1788–95). It has been immortalised by Fanny Burney and Macaulay. Hastings presented, we are told, a sorry figure, frail and emaciated. This did not soften the heart of Edmund Burke whose fanatical eloquence was carried to extreme lengths: 'I charge him with fraud and abuse, treachery and robbery! I charge him with cruelties unheard of and devastations almost without a name! . .' and so on.

After seven years Hastings was acquitted by a large majority on each of the 16 questions that was put to the vote. Burke, whose final argument for the prosecution had lasted nine days, was not surprisingly cynical about the result. 'As to the acquittal,' he wrote to Lord Loughborough in 1796, 'that it was total I was surprised at; that it should be so in a good measure I expected from the incredible corruption of the time.'

The greatest number of Lords that sat at any one time during the trial was 168. Usually there were from 30 to 50. There had been in all 180 changes from death or other causes during the proceedings. Whether one looked at it from the point of view of Hastings or Burke, it was a caricature of justice.

While the impeachment of Lord Melville in 1805 was to be the last such proceeding, it took a significant time for this fact to be appreciated. There was, for instance, talk of impeaching Palmerston in the 1860s. So, too, the Lords took seriously their responsibilities for the felony trials of their own members. The peers, moreover, maintained their strong interest in important appeals. In 1698 some 107 peers were present at the hearing of the appeal in *Bertie v. Lord Falkland*: 13 peers dissented in the election case of *Ashby v. White* (1703).

In the years 1712–14 not only did the Lords reverse the lower courts in almost a third of the cases heard, but the lay peers were responsible for dividing the House twice. In the *Douglas-Hamilton Case* in 1769, 107 peers attended and six dissented from Mansfield's opinion, while in *Bishop of London v. Ffytche* (1783), the episcopal bench succeeded in reversing the lower court 19–18, by persuading the House not to follow the advice of the judges who had been summoned.

But by 1844, in practice if not in theory, all this judicial decision-making by legally unqualified persons had vanished. The pressure for reform came about from three sources, the movement towards democracy still in its infancy, the Benthamite demand for efficiency at all costs, and the stream of Scottish Appeals which proved insatiable. Various changes were effected. An Order of the House early in 1824 provided that with the exception of those able to claim exemption, all peers should be liable to be drafted to hear appeals at the rate of three peers a day. The rules for balloting were carefully laid down, including a £50 fine for non-attendance, and the rota of lords was published at the beginning of each session. The new system might on the face of it have strengthened the position of the lay peers in the decision-making process. But in fact it made it obvious that the lay peers were mere cyphers. If a case continued for three days, it was heard on the first day by Lords A and B, on the second day by Lords C and D, on the third by Lords E and F. When the judgement came to be delivered, the lords present, besides the Lord Chancellor who had sat throughout, would be Lords G and H. This kind of nonsense could not continue indefinitely. In 1833 the judicial functions of the Privy Council had passed to a judicial committee. 'By 1833, then, both the House of Lords and the Privy

Council had taken on the more obvious guise of courts and were becoming increasingly independent of the legislative and executive organs whose names they bore.' (Stevens).

The decisive change was confirmed in 1844 in connection with the trial of Daniel O'Connell, the renowned Irish leader who was convicted in the Dublin Court of conspiracy. He appealed by Writ of Error to the House of Lords. The hearing came on before five law lords – Brougham, Lyndhurst, Denman, Cottenham, and Campbell; the 12 common law judges were also summoned to attend for their advice. The majority of the judges confirmed the decision of the Dublin Court. Two of the law lords also upheld the conviction, but the other three, i.e. the majority, were for reversing it and for allowing the 'Writ of Error'. Various lay peers now attempted to vote with the minority of the law lords, i.e. against O'Connell. A general debate broke out. The Earl of Stradbroke in particular was anxious to deliver a speech. Peel, however, the Prime Minister, sent Lord Wharncliffe, Lord President of the Privy Council down to the House to prevent a crisis. He counselled the House not to divide 'when the opinion of the law lords had been already given upon it.' He boldly stated that 'the law lords constitute the Court of Appeal.' He very much feared that if 'noble lords unlearned in the law interfered to decide such questions by their votes, the outcome would be that the authority of the House of Lords as a court of justice would be greatly lessened.'

There was much anger among the Tory peers who had wanted to secure the conviction of O'Connell. From 1844, however, a convention was established. It appears that lay peers may have been recruited to make up a quorum as late as the 1860s but after 1844 they had no effective vote. Even today, it would seem that lay peers have a legal right to vote, whatever that may mean. The last claimant who attempted to vote was Lord Denman, who purported to vote in *Bradlaugh v. Clarke* (1883). His vote was ignored by the Lord Chancellor and also in the official law report.

The elimination of the lay peers did not however solve all the problems involved in the establishment of an effective appeals machinery. The Act of 1876 already referred to established the judicial role of the House of Lords on a firm basis. Stevens remarks

133

that two years earlier the House of Lords as a judicial body had appeared to be doomed. In effect, however, the new court was now quite obviously separate from the House of Lords as a legislative body. Stevens discusses at length the performance of the House of Lords as a judicial body from 1876 to 1976. He is concerned in particular with the question of how far it was consciously or unconsciously creative, that is, not only a law-interpreting but a law-making body. For my part, I would not try to improve on the words of Lord Radcliffe, a Lord of Appeal (law lord) from 1949 to 1964, who was much used by government for every kind of official enquiry: 'There was never a more sterile controversy than that upon the question whether a judge makes law. Of course he does. How can he help it? . . . Judicial law is always a reinterpretation of principles in the light of new combinations of facts. . . . Judges do not reverse principles, once well established, but they do modify them, extend them, restrict them and even deny their application to the combination in hand.'

The issue would take us far outside the confines of the present book. It must arise in the last resort under any constitutional system. The peculiar feature of our British arrangement is that the Lord Chancellor, himself a judge, and in that capacity, supposed to be far removed from party politics, is a member of the Cabinet, a leading Government spokesman in the House of Lords. (He is also Speaker of the House, but that is a purely formal office.) He is also head of the Judiciary. To him falls the all-important task of appointing the judges. This strange arrangement is a product of history. No one would recommend it to a young country setting up a new constitution.

In my own time, I have been aware of many occasions when the conflict of interest and disinterest has been too much for the Lord Chancellor to bear. For example, at the time of Suez. If I take an extreme example from twentieth-century history for the purposes of illustration, it must not be thought to be typical. In 1901 the Lord Chancellor in the Conservative government was Lord Halsbury, highly respected, but rightly considered an extreme conservative. The question at issue was the basic one of whether Trade Unions were liable for loss arising from a strike. At first instance the judge, a

Halsbury appointee, not only granted an injunction in favour of the railway company, but under the head of 'further relief' he held the officers of the union personally liable for damages for inducing their members to breach a contract. The Court of Appeal reversed the decision. Stevens describes the sequel without mincing his words. 'To the astonishment of the legal profession and the dismay of the unions, the House held that a Trade Union could be sued in such a situation.' He accuses Halsbury in terms of having arranged for a sympathetic panel of law lords. He continues: 'The case must bear the distinction of being one of the politically unhappiest decisions that the House ever rendered.' It permanently weakened the reputation of the law lords. ... The unions threw their weight behind the Liberals, the Labour Party and the Lib–Labs in the ensuing General Election. There followed the Trades Disputes Act of 1906, which put the unions largely outside the ambit of the legal system.

Moving on to the present time one is conscious that law lords are likely to be conservative-minded. Their age and their profession inclines them that way, though there have been notable exceptions such as Lords Chancellor Gardiner and Elwyn-Jones. The complete integrity and formidable power of intellect of the judges has never been questioned in my time. We would be honoured if they mixed with us more freely outside the Chamber. The best-known and best-loved of them has, for many years, been Lord Denning who insists on putting into practice, wherever possible, his deeply held conceptions of justice.

CHAPTER VIII

1905–1911

The Showdown

We now come to the most traumatic period in the history of the House of Lords. Between 1906 and 1911 a head-on collision first threatened and then occurred between the House of Lords and the Liberal Government. On 10 August the Lords, by a narrow majority, accepted defeat. Their absolute veto over legislation coming from the House of Commons was removed. In its place the Lords were accorded a delaying power of two years. The Lords gave way for one reason only. Asquith, the Liberal Prime Minister, had obtained from the new King, George V a promise to create enough peers to pass the Bill in the Lords. The majority of the peers, overwhelmingly conservative, had reacted like the members of any other threatened institution. They saw it as at once their interest and their duty to 'repel boarders' all the more because the boarders in question were politically and socially anathema. The Conservative leaders must be given credit for a more calculating strategy. It seems now to have been similar to that of Lord Salisbury, the former Prime Minister, described above. They asserted a moral and political right to hold up unwelcome legislation which had not been approved by public opinion as expressed in a general election.

Throughout these hectic and confusing years the more far-sighted Conservatives were concerned at all times to improve the credibility of the House of Lords, with a view to their winning public approval at election time. With that in mind they were ready to sacrifice some degree of the hereditary principle in order to improve their standing with the public. Hence their various schemes for reforming the Upper House. We must say a few words about past discussion of this subject. In 1884 and again in 1888, the Earl of

Rosebery, a Liberal peer, proposed that Select Committees should be appointed to consider how the efficiency of the House might be improved, but on both occasions the motions were defeated. In 1888, the Earl of Dunraven, a Conservative peer, introduced a far-reaching House of Lords (Constitution) Bill, but withdrew it before Second Reading. In the House of Commons, too, reform of the Lords was debated during this period; in 1886 and 1888, for instance, the Commons discussed resolutions condemning any hereditary right to a seat in the legislature. Neither resolution was carried. As already noted, Gladstone would have liked a dissolution after the overwhelming defeat of his Home Rule Bill in 1893, making reform of the Lords the primary issue. He was turned down on that occasion by his colleagues, but reform of the Lords was thenceforward a Liberal concern, though it did not have much of a priority.

In the years we are now considering, 1905–1911, a number of initiatives in the direction of reform came to nothing. In 1907, Lord Newton, a Conservative peer, introduced a Bill which would have ended the automatic right of an hereditary peer to a seat in the House of Lords. The Bill was withdrawn, and a Select Committee of the House, chaired by the Earl of Rosebery, was appointed in lieu to consider proposals for reform. When the Committee reported in 1908, it echoed Lord Newton's Bill by concluding that 'it was undesirable that the possession of a Peerage should of itself give the right to sit and vote in the House of Lords'. It is noteworthy that 80 years later this attitude, accepted by a majority of Conservatives, has still not yet been enshrined in the British Constitution. The great majority of the members of the House of Lords are still entitled to sit there because of their inherited titles. (But see above, page 22.)

In 1911, the Marquess of Lansdowne, the Leader of the Opposition in the Lords, introduced a Bill proposing a reconstituted House of Lords, consisting mainly of indirectly elected members. However, the Bill was dropped when the Government pressed on with its own Parliament Bill. Lord Newton, in his life of Lansdowne published in 1929, said of House of Lords reform that it now seemed doubtful 'when anything ever will be done'. He continued, 'The fact is that the desire for reform is confined to a small section of politicians who look further ahead than the ordinary man; but they have no substantial backing in the country, and the House of Commons has no desire to increase the efficiency of the Second Chamber.'

The Liberal Cabinet which came into power under Campbell-Bannerman at the beginning of 1906, had behind it a large majority in the House of Commons, following the General Election. But there was a majority even more pronounced against it in the House of Lords. 'At the beginning of the first session of the new Parliament there were 602 peers, including twenty-five bishops, who were entitled to take part in the proceedings of the House of Lords. Of these only eighty-eight described themselves as Liberals – and this number included a few who were as uncertain in their support of the Government as was Lord Rosebery. One hundred and twenty-four were Liberal Unionists and 355 were Conservatives, leaving only thirty-five, including fourteen bishops and a number of Princes of the Blood, who gave themselves no political label. The nominal Unionist majority was 391, a preponderance still more decisive than that of the Government in the new House of Commons.' (Roy Jenkins, *Mr Balfour's Poodle*).

Balfour, the Conservative leader, made no secret of his intention that whoever was in office the Conservative Party would remain in control. He announced in an election speech on 15 January 1906 that it was the duty of everyone to see that 'the Great Unionist Party should still control whether in power or whether in opposition the destinies of this great Empire.' The Conservative majority in the Lords soon revealed themselves, in conjunction with their colleagues in the Commons, as determined to stand no nonsense from the Liberal Government, however large its majority elsewhere. They got to work with a will. Over a three-year period 'no measure other than a Money Bill had passed onto the Statute Book in anything like its original form, unless on the third reading in the Commons it had secured the acquiescence of Balfour, the Conservative leader.' (Roy Jenkins, *Mr Balfour's Poodle*).

It is worth our spending a moment on two Bills in particular, the Education Bill and a Licensing Bill. The Education Bill of 1906 was singled out for special commendation in the King's Speech at the opening of the 1906 session. It was intended to remedy some of the grievances felt by the non-conformists as a result of the Conservative Education Bill of 1902. It was greeted with a storm of protest, not only from the Unionist Party but also from the Anglican and Roman Catholic Churches. The present writer, a Roman Catholic, is not likely to feel any retrospective sympathy for the measure. Nevertheless here was a Bill which had behind it beyond any question a strong popular mandate so soon after the General Election. The Conservatives collectively wrecked it. In the House of Commons it was bogged down in Committee for 20 parliamentary days. It needed an extensive use of the guillotine to push it through. In the House of Lords the Bill was amended so totally that it finished up a completely different article. The House of Commons voted by 416 to 107 to reject the Lords' amendment. The Lords in their turn carried a motion by 132 to 52 that 'this House do insist upon the amendments which the Commons have disagreed.' The deadlock was now complete.

The Prime Minister, Campbell-Bannerman, and the Liberal Government were forced to abandon the Bill. Some of the words of the Prime Minister are worth quoting. 'The resources of the British Constitution are not wholly exhausted, the resources of the House of Commons are not exhausted, and I say with conviction that a way must be found, a way will be found, by which the will of the people expressed through their elected representatives in this House will be made to prevail.'

The Lords continued to sabotage the elaborate Liberal programme of social reform in ruthless fashion. Finally, the Licensing Bill, which was intended to bring about a reduction in the number of public houses, was rejected on 27 November 1908 on its second reading in the Lords by a vote of 272 to 96 – a large vote then or now. A third Education Bill had also perished at the hands of the Lords during the year.

Mr Ponsonby

It was obvious that the Liberal Government could not lie down under such destructive opposition. The Liberal leaders had plenty of trouble with the Opposition but they were not being given too easy a ride by their own supporters. For example, on 22 February 1909, the Liberal MP Mr Arthur Ponsonby proposed that 'it is necessary that the power of the other House to alter or reject Bills passed by this House should be so restricted by law as to secure that within the limits of a single Parliament the final decision of the Commons shall prevail.'

As Private Secretary to Campbell-Bannerman he had persuaded his chief that it was essential to divorce the issues of powers and competition to solve the problem of the House of Lords.

Arthur Ponsonby had impeccable aristocratic credentials as a scion of perhaps the most famous Irish political family and the son of the most famous of Queen Victoria's Private Secretaries. He expressed a sense of deep disappointment that the Government had not already acted in this matter and that it was left to him to take an initiative. 'I am quite aware,' he said, 'that in a great many remarks which I shall have to make this afternoon I shall receive cheers and jeers from the honourable members opposite. But I note with satisfaction that, as time goes on, the once hilarious laughter that greeted the mention of this subject is becoming a little more hollow in tone and a little more nervous and hysterical.'

'It is,' he said, 'exceedingly difficult to restrain one's language in dealing with the House of Lords.' He promised, however, to do his best. His language in fact would seem 70 years later reasonably stark. 'The principle of hereditary legislators,' he said, 'will not hold for a moment because it is really not defended anywhere.' No longer did people generally take the view the peers were descended in a straight line from people who came over with William the Conqueror. 'We all of us know now that they are quite modern creations. Peers are people very much like anybody else except that they have had the advantage of a public school education.'

For his part, the aristocracy seemed to have had a certain distinction which now was fast fading away. However, 'they seemed to retain,' as I understand his argument, 'a certain illegitimate influence in the country.' He felt sure that 'our legislation will be rejected, will be mutilated, and will be emasculated,' unless drastic steps were taken on the lines of his amendment.

The rest of the debate was not remarkable. Asquith, the Prime Minister, replied adroitly in his best wait-and-see style, which some still possess today. In effect he sympathised with the aspirations of Ponsonby but cautioned him and his followers against precipitate action. The issue in the end would be taken to the people. But 'the cause is not likely to be jeopardised nor the issue in the long run less wisely decided because it is presented in all its aspects after full deliberation and consideration to the tribunal of public opinion.' In the event the ayes, that is the party of Ponsonby, were defeated by 47 votes to 225, Asquith and the other members of the government voting against him. Ponsonby's reactions can be imagined. In 1914 we find him bringing in a Bill to abolish the hereditary element in the House of Lords. It became a casualty of the war.

Many years later he emerged as the Leader of the Labour Party in the House of Lords. I heard him speak with feline grace in a debate on Sanctions at the Labour Party Conference in 1935. He was on the left of his party, Liberal or Labour, to the end. At the moment of writing, his grandson is the much esteemed Chief Whip of the Labour peers.

Against this background came the introduction of Lloyd George's Budget in April 1909. The details need not be entered into here. Roy Jenkins considers that the introduction of super-tax was the most pregnant with social change. There is no doubt however that the land taxes aroused the most controversies. There were three of these. The first provided for a tax of 20% on the unearned increment in land values, which was to be paid either when the land was sold or when it passed at death. The second provided for a capital tax of $\frac{1}{2}$d in the £ on the value of undeveloped land and minerals; and the third for a 10% reversion duty on any benefit which came to a lessor at the end of a lease. These taxes were to bring in only £500,000 in the current year, but their yield was expected to increase considerably in subsequent years.

All through the summer the public controversy raged in the House of Commons and elsewhere. It has never been clear whether Lloyd George, in particular, desired to provoke the Lords into a rejection of his Budget. Whether he did or did not, he stoked the fires enthusiastically with wonderful rhetoric. On 17 September the Prime Minister, Asquith, was still purporting to suppose that 'Amendment by the House of Lords is out of the question'. He went on, 'Rejection by the House of Lords [of the Budget] is equally out of the question. Is this issue going to be raised? If it is carried it will bring with it in its train consequences which he would be a bold man to forecast or foresee. That way revolution lies.' It was common knowledge that the peers had not rejected a Finance Bill for more than 250 years. Rejection of such a measure was obviously on a different footing from rejection of new legislation. It would stop in its tracks the government of the day and force willy-nilly a General Election.

A little background seems to be necessary here. Pike, writing in 1894, had commented 'the limitation of the power of Lords when legislating on money bills is a subject with regard to which our early history is obscure.' By the time of the Restoration, however, the Commons had taken up a dogmatic position. In 1661 the Commons objected to a Bill sent down to them from the Lords and having for its object the paving of the streets of Westminster. They said that 'it went to lay a charge upon the people,' and that 'it was a privilege inherent in their House that Bills of that nature should first be considered there.' They then sent up a Bill of their own, but the Lords amended it by the insertion of a clause, which the Commons would not accept because, as they said, the amendment infringed their privileges. The Lords did not admit that they had no power in such a matter as this, and produced some precedents which they considered to be in their favour. As neither side would give way, no legislation could be effected.

In 1671 the Commons resolved that 'in all aid given to the King by the Commons the rate of tax ought not to be altered by the Lords'. In

1678 they resolved, 'that all aids and supplies, and aids to His Majesty in Parliament, are the sole gift of the Commons; and all Bills for the granting of any such aids and supplies ought to begin with the Commons; and that it is the undoubted and sole right of the Commons to direct, limit, and appoint, in such Bills, the ends, purposes, considerations, conditions, limitations, and qualifications of such grants, which ought not to be changed or altered by the House of Lords.'

Pike points out that this resolution did not in itself affect the power of the Lords to *reject* the money Bill although it denied them the power of *initiating* or *altering*.

Writing in 1894 he informs us that 'the proceedings of later times were long regulated in the main by this most important resolution of the year 1678.' He was of course well aware by that time of the events of 1860. In that year the Commons sent up to the Lords a Bill for the repeal of Acts imposing duties upon paper. The Lords rejected it; the Commons reasserted their rights in a series of resolutions. One was 'that the right of granting aids and supplies to the Crown is in the Commons alone.' In another, though it was admitted that the Lords had on previous occasions rejected money Bills, it was declared that the exercise of the power of rejection was 'justly regarded' by the House of Commons 'with peculiar jealousy, as affecting the right of the Commons to grant the supplies, and to provide the ways and means for the service of the year.' A third was to the effect 'that to guard, for the future, against an undue exercise of that power by the Lords, and to secure to the Commons their rightful control over taxation and supply' the House of Commons 'has in its own hands the power so to impose and remit taxes, and to frame Bills of Supply, that the right of the Commons as to the matter, manner, measure and time, may be maintained inviolate'.

Against this background the rejection of the Liberal Budget of 1909 by the House of Lords would have seemed unthinkable a few years earlier. But the House of Lords had now got the bit between its teeth. The by-elections had been running heavily against the Government. The Lords calculated, wrongly as it turns out, but not absurdly, that one more push, a push which landed the Liberals inevitably in a General Election, would see them hurled from power.

Hence on 10 November 1909, before the Budget reached the Lords, the Opposition had decided to throw it out.

The debate which began on 22 November and lasted for five days is of exceptional interest. Not because there was any doubt about the outcome (unlike the debate which was to follow in August 1911) but because of the constitutional position as it was seen by the various spokesmen. Lansdowne, the Conservative leader, announced that he was not going to 'attempt any elaboration of the historical argument illustrating the long controversy between the two Houses of Parliament as to the respective privileges. Those controversies are necessarily somewhat inconclusive because obviously each House has a right to its own opinions and the opinion of one House cannot of itself prevail over the opinion of the other.'

He insisted, however, that even if the claim of the House of Commons were taken at its highest, 'you will not find that that claim bars the right of the Lords to *reject* a Bill of this kind.' He proceeded, 'I trust that I have said enough to show your lordships that the question before you is not whether you *can* reject this Bill but whether you *ought to* reject this Bill, a wholly different thing.' Not surprisingly he denounced the Bill as disastrous to the country.

His social and economic arguments do not concern us now except to say that they were shared by the vast majority of the House. Lord Lansdowne was at pains to argue that it was 'idle to talk of the Bill as being an ordinary Budget Bill to which the ordinary treatment of the annual Budget Bill would of necessity apply.' If in other words they were entitled to reject an ordinary Budget they were *a fortiori* entitled to reject this horrible departure.

Lord Crewe had moved the Second Reading of the Finance Bill. The first speech made for the Government came from the Lord Chancellor, Lord Loreburn. He began by pointing out that Lord Lansdowne had said hardly anything of the extreme gravity from the constitutional point of view of the step which he was introducing.

'If I am asked,' he went on, 'whether you can do it lawfully, according to law, I answer undeniably yes; and the best test of that is that a Court of law would not give effect to any tax which had been refused by the House of Lords and was not ultimately embodied in an Act of Parliament. But if I am asked whether this House can do it constitutionally, I say – in my opinion, no.'

He asked what would happen if all the estates of the realm were to carry out in freedom all the powers which the law entrusted to them. 'The Crown has enormous powers and some of them for centuries have not been used. Those who wish to govern the country must look not just to the letter of the law but even more to custom, usage, convention, which by inveterate practice had so modified the hard law itself that we were governed more by custom in this country than we were even by the law'.

Reading the debate now one senses that he was on strong ground here but had more difficulty in defeating the criticism that non-financial matters had been 'tacked on' to the Budget. Lord Halsbury, the veteran ex-Chancellor, speaking as the leader of the die-hards during this period, rejected any suggestion that he and his colleagues were violating the constitution. He asked with extreme indignation which part of the constitution was being violated. He laid great stress on the fact that 'the whole bundle of measures' were being taken together and that any existing tradition about not rejecting the Budget did not apply.

He finished on a note of defiance. There had been suggestions that the House of Lords would suffer if they rejected the Budget. 'One thing at all events I will say – that, if I was to be supposed to be actuated one way or the other because I was threatened with extinction and made to suppose that I would be deprived of all privileges, I would not value a seat in a House which would yield to such a paltry apprehension.'

In this atmosphere there could be no possible meeting of minds. The Lord Chancellor, Lord Loreburn, had told the House that the action contemplated by the Opposition was 'a direct invasion both of the prerogative of the Crown and the privileges of the House of Commons. . . . To the Crown belongs the supreme authority overall checked by the doctrine of ministerial responsibility and by the power of the House of Commons to refuse to supply. To the House of Commons belongs control over the Purse . . . to the Lords belongs the supreme jurisdiction in the administration of justice – surely of itself a noble attribute together with a full share in all legislation except finance. This long established balance in the constitution would be fatally undermined if the Opposition had their way.'

But the vast majority of the peers would not listen. When it came to the votes the Contents were 75 and the Not Contents 350. Balfour of Burleigh was almost the only dissenting Unionist who voted for the Bill. The great majority of bishops, including the Archbishop of Canterbury, abstained, although the Archbishop of York and three others voted for the Government. The Bishop of Lincoln voted with the Opposition.

A dissolution of Parliament followed automatically. The Government had been refused Supply and could not have carried on even if they had wished to. It was this which made the action of the Lords so provocative, for good or ill. They had decided that a Parliament elected by the people must seek immediately a new mandate.

Asquith responded immediately. On 2 December he moved that 'the action of the House of Lords in refusing to pass into law the financial provision made by this House for the service of the year is a breach of the Constitution and a usurpation of the rights of the Commons.'

The House of Commons was immediately dissolved – 'at the earliest possible moment we shall ask the constituencies of the country to declare that the organ and voice of the free people of this country is to be found in the elected representatives of the nation.' A resolution to that effect supported by both the Irish and the Labour Party was carried by 349 votes to 134.

The result of the election was bound to be crucial. If the Conservatives prevailed, they would be able to claim a classical vindication of the Salisbury principle that the Lords were entitled to appeal from the Commons and the government of the day to the people. If the Liberals won, they would be in a strong position to restrict the delaying power of the Lords. In the event the result must be described as a draw. The Liberals lost many seats, though not as many as they feared or their opponents hoped. They finished up roughly equal to the Conservatives. With the support of the Labour Party and the Irish Nationalists, but only with such support, they could carry the day in the House of Commons.

Obviously they meant business. No one could say what would have happened in 1910 if Edward VII had not died unexpectedly on 6 May. There was a general disposition to seek common ground if such existed in the new reign. By 10 November the attempt at compromise had failed. The Liberal leaders had put forward what was called the Ripon plan, which since 1907 had been under discussion as an alternative to Campbell-Bannerman's proposal to restrict the veto. Under Campbell-Bannerman's plan the suspensory veto of the Lords could conceivably have limited the period of the veto to little more than six months. Under the Ripon plan in the event of difference between the two Houses the disputed measure would be finally settled by a joint vote in which the House of Commons would sit as a body, but the House of Lords would be represented by a delegation of 100 members. The break-down of the Conference was not due to disagreement over the principle of this plan but to the inability of the two delegations to agree on the special treatment to be accorded Home Rule Bills. Balfour's note on the Conference seems to be an accurate summary: 'Subsequently the Government proposed a compromise, viz, that a general election should intervene on the next occasion on which a Home Rule Bill, having passed the House of Commons, was rejected by the House of Lords – but only on this one occasion; and that Home Rule Bills if introduced afterwards should be treated like ordinary bills.' The point of division seemed a narrow one, but the Unionist Party were passionately committed to thwarting all plans for Home Rule and the Liberals, if with less passion, were just as deeply committed to keeping faith with their Irish Nationalist allies.

Another general election was inevitable. It duly took place in December 1910. The result was almost exactly the same as earlier in the year. There was now no possibility of compromise. A Bill to reform the House of Lords was introduced to the House of Commons. It restricted the Lords' veto to two years. It came up for a Second Reading in the House of Lords on 23 May 1911. The Lords gave it a Second Reading, but introduced and carried a series of damaging amendments.

Everyone was by now aware of the crucial question: would Asquith be able and willing to secure from the King a promise to create sufficient peers to carry the Bill through the House of Lords? Asquith had a curious passion for keeping his cards close to his chest till the last possible moment. He had in fact secured the requisite assurances from the King before the last election. Now at last he showed his hand. He wrote on 20 July to the Conservative leaders Balfour and Lansdowne to warn them that in the last resort he would be compelled to advise the King to exercise his prerogative 'to secure the passing into law of the Bill in substantially the same form in which it had left the House of Commons.' That would mean the rejection of the Lords' amendments. Asquith was able to add this telling conclusion: 'His Majesty was pleased to signify that he would consider it his duty to accept and act on that advice.' The Unionists soon found themselves poignantly split.

The Unionist peers were hurriedly summoned to a meeting at Lansdowne House on 21 July 1911 at which the arguments for and against continued resistance were forcibly deployed. Lord Newton, usually a laudatory biographer, criticises Lansdowne for failing to give a lead, though he (Lansdowne) had already decided, it now seems, in favour of abstention. Lord Halsbury, the former Lord Chancellor, Lord Salisbury, and others vigorously denounced any idea of surrender.

Frantic wirepulling now took place among the Unionists on all sides of the argument. The role of their leaders was somewhat ignominious. They were horrified at the prospect of the creation of several hundred peers. They were well aware that the Bill would pass into law with or without such a creation. They were not however prepared to recommend support for the Bill – 'as such a proceeding would have caused intense indignation and accentuated the split in the party' (Newton's *Life of Lansdowne*). The Government could not count on more than about 75 supporters and it seems quite likely that the diehards, led by Halsbury, could surpass that figure.

Somehow or other a moderate number of peers who were ready to earn the title of Judas by actually voting for the Bill, were collected in the Carlton Club. On the face of it Lansdowne played no part in mobilising them. Credit has been given, for example by the well-informed Roy Jenkins, to Lord Curzon. He certainly incurred enough odium from the diehards. Since then one learned scholar has demonstrated that Lord Newton was the architect. He in his turn has been refuted by rival scholars. They have satisfied themselves that it was really Lord Cromer, a man of much higher standing than Lord Newton, whose influence produced enough 'traitors' to serve the purposes of the Government and the Unionist leaders.

9–10 August 1911

The debate on the Parliament Bill which began in the House of Lords on 9 August 1911, and was due to conclude on the following day, was unique in the annals of either House of Parliament. There has never been a major occasion when the outcome was so uncertain at the beginning and when the issue remained in such doubt to the very end. On the preceding day, 8 August, a vote of censure had been carried on the Government by 283 to 68. In the Commons, where, as in the Lords, the voting had been on strict party lines, the Vote of Censure had been rejected by 353 to 245. But for reasons explained above these results threw no light on what would happen when it came to a vote in the Lords.

The two best accounts of this are in the reminiscences of Lord Morley who bore the brunt of the defence of the Bill, and in the *Life* by Wilson Fox of Lord Halsbury who led the resistance of the diehards. It is worth recalling that London was sweltering under conditions of intense heat. The mercury recorded 97° in the shade, the highest temperature for 70 years. Morley's general comment on the debate was as detached as one might expect from the biographer than from the party leader. The mood, he wrote, was plain honest anger. The point *was not to convince the opponent, but to run him through*. The two warring Unionist sections were at least as incensed against one another as against ministers. The situation forced the position of the Crown into agitating and dangerous prominence, and this prominence naturally inflamed both resentment against Government and sympathetic concern for the young Sovereign.

Morley himself, opening the debate, did little more 'than kick the ball into play', leaving the official Unionists and the die-hards to fight it out. The hopelessness of resistance was the main theme from Lord Lansdowne with which the debate began.

'We know,' said the leader of the Conservative peers, 'or at least I know, that we have no means of preventing this Bill finding a place on the Statute Book.' To cause the Government – and with them the Crown – to adopt the alternative of creating a large number of peers was an 'odious alternative'. And it would not in the end be effective. Lansdowne gave a clear lead in favour of a policy of abstention. This in itself, however, could not solve the Government's problem. Halsbury came next, receiving, according to his biographer, a tremendous reception. The fine veteran did his stuff along predictable lines. He finished with the words, 'I have nothing more to say, except that nothing in the world will induce me to vote for a Bill or to abstain from voting against a Bill which I believe to be wrong and immoral and a scandalous example of legislation.' The speeches that followed were in Morley's phrasing 'in the strain of altercation, hot or cold, rather than serious contributions.' As the day wore on, Morley became aware that a large number of the Unionists could not bring themselves to believe that the threat of a large creation of peers was genuine. They continued to persuade themselves that it was a gigantic bluff. Morley, not always regarded as a man of action, acted promptly. He secured permission from the King for a form of words which he used next morning and which should have removed any doubts about the Government's intentions.

Nevertheless the issue remained in doubt up till the end. The speech of the Archbishop of Canterbury, though it only lasted three or four minutes, had probably more influence than any other. He admitted that the course of the debate had made him change his mind – and what had produced this effect? It was the callousness – he had almost said levity – with which some noble Lords seemed to contemplate the creation of 500 new peers; 'a course of action that would make this House, and indeed the country, the laughing-stock of the British Dominions beyond the seas, and of those foreign countries whose constitutional life and progress had been largely modelled on our own.' The Archbishop had intended to abstain but now he would support the Bill. So direct a criticism of a large number of noble lords was and is somewhat rare in the House but it certainly affected the voting.

Lord Curzon winding up for the Opposition, managed to cause a good deal of annoyance. This extract from Hansard provides an example.

> Earl Curzon of Kedleston: 'Let us realise what is before us.'
>
> The Marquess of Bristol: 'It is because 400 Peers are going to run away to night.'
>
> Earl Curzon of Kedleston: 'I would sooner run away with the Duke of Wellington than stand with the noble Lord.'
>
> The Marquess of Bristol: 'I would rather fight with Nelson at Copenhagen than run away with the noble Earl.'
>
> Earl Curzon of Kedleston: 'I do not wish to get involved in a controversy with the noble Lord.'

Curzon seems on the whole to have been a liability to his side. Rosebery was of no more positive value. The former Prime Minister, still a commanding orator, who had made the subject his own in past times, made the ambivalent kind of speech which had become the hallmark of his later years. The Bill, as he had made clear already, was abhorrent to him. Nevertheless he would personally vote with the Government. He cut a sorry figure after so many glorious performances. And so they came to the division.

'As one,' wrote Morley, 'who has voted in a thousand divisions, I felt that the universal strain tonight was far more intense than any of them.' Even in the middle of the division 'the undaunted leader of the diehards whispered to the ministerial teller, "There, I knew that we should beat you." But when the votes were counted, there was a majority for the government of 17. The voting was, Contents: 131; Not Contents: 114. The Government's own supporters were only 80 out of the 131. The Unionists (to whom the word Judas was applied by the diehards) were 37, the prelates 13. Wilson Fox in writing from the Halsbury point of view, refers to 'last minute defections from the diehards to the Lansdowne abstainers'. But the

votes of the 13 bishops and any laymen influenced by the Archbishop of Canterbury were the crucial factors.

It is amusing to look at pages 390–395 of the House of Lords
Journal for 10 August 1911. We are told that after Prayers the Order
of the Day was read for the Second Reading of Watson's Divorce
Bill. Other Bills of similar importance or unimportance followed.
The Newcastle-upon-Tyne Corporation Bill was read a third time.
Various messages were brought from the House of Commons
regarding such Bills as The Chiswick Urban District Council Bill,
The Halifax Corporation Bill, The London County Council
(Money) Bill, The Margam Urban District Council Bill, The
Rotherham Corporation Bill and The St. Helens Corporation Bill.
Various measures of similar character, occupying in all two and a
half large pages of the Journal, were then disposed of.

Finally, 'The Order of the Day being read for resuming the
adjourned Debate on the Motion made yesterday, "That the
Commons' Reasons for disagreeing to certain of the Amendments
made by the Lords to The Parliament Bill, and the Commons'
consequential Amendment made to the Bill, be now taken into
consideration".'

Only about half a page is occupied with a summary of the debate
and its outcome which I have already recorded above. What is
striking and quite without precedent in my personal experience is
what follows – the record of the division.

It is in accord with an older practice and is headed 'Dissentient'. It
sets out under ten headings the reasons why the 15 signatories
desire to place on record their reasons for disagreement with the
decision reached by the House. Only the first and the last reasons
can be quoted here.

1 It destroys the balance of the Constitution
10 The whole transaction tends to bring discredit on our
   country and its institutions.

One rubs one's eyes as one reads the name of the first signatory,
Rosebery. Lord Rosebery had voted for the proposal which he now
announced would bring discredit on the country and its institutions.

CHAPTER IX

1911–1945

The House in Transition

The years between 1911 and 1945 are not very interesting to the historian of the House of Lords. The 1911 Parliament Act was not intended to be more than temporary. The Conservative Opposition used to the full the delaying powers left to them, in relation to the Bill disestablishing the Church of Wales, and the Home Rule Bill which was enacted in 1914 under the Parliament Act procedure. The retention of the delaying power played its part in bringing about the extreme tensions which were resolved only temporarily by the outbreak of war in August 1914.

In 1917 a conference under the chairmanship of Lord Bryce made its report on the functions and changes appropriate to a reformed House, of whose members three-quarters would be elected indirectly by MPs on a regional basis, with the remaining quarter chosen by a joint standing committee of both Houses, with a proportion of hereditary peers and bishops. But the members of the conference were not in full agreement. The government was preoccupied with the war and no action followed.

I need only mention here that reform of the House of Lords was mentioned in the King's Speeches of 1920, 1921 and 1922. In 1922 the Government put forward resolutions of its own. In 1927 the Conservative government of the day put forward further proposals. Private Members' Bills were introduced by Conservative peers – in 1929, 1933 and 1935. A Bill favouring life peers was withdrawn before Second Reading in 1929. Both the Marquess of Salisbury's Parliament (Reform) Bill and Lord Rockley's Life Peers Bill were read a second time in 1934 and 1935, but were not proceeded with in committee and Lord Rankeillour's Parliament Act 1911 (Amendment Bill) was withdrawn before Second Reading in 1935.

It is noteworthy that all or almost all the pressure for reforming the House of Lords came from the Conservative side. There was an underlying, an almost desperate, desire to give the House of Lords the kind of rational and defensible basis that would enable it to play a much more significant part in the democratic age. There was no enthusiasm on the Left for any such tinkering which, in the last resort, left a decisive role to hereditary peers.

By and large the Lords debates during this period while distinguished in theme were not particularly dramatic. The Conservative majority was too large to make that likely. One debate, however, taking place on 14, 15 and 16 December 1921 has always intrigued me for more reasons than one. It was a debate in which the House were asked to express their approval in principle for the agreement usually called the Anglo-Irish Treaty reached between the British and Irish representatives just over a week earlier. It happens that I myself wrote about 50 years ago a full-length study of the events leading to the Anglo–Irish Treaty, which has remained a standard work. That is one reason but not the main one for my interest in this particular debate.

When I was an undergraduate at Oxford I became a great friend of Freddie Furneaux, son of the first Earl of Birkenhead. I spent many weekends at their house near Oxford. There was golf in the morning, tennis in the afternoon and riding between tea and dinner. Dinner provided an opportunity for anecdotes from our host, the former F. E. Smith, of a quality that I have never known equalled. 'F.E.' had been a rising Conservative politician before 1914 and had become known as a 'Galloper Smith' the Principal Aide to Edward Carson, the Ulster leader. Carson had gone to the very verge of revolution in seeking to prevent the imposition of Home Rule on Ulster. F. E. Smith had been at his elbow throughout, but by December 1921 Smith had become Lord Chancellor Birkenhead, a principal architect of the Irish Treaty. Carson, who regarded this as a monstrous betrayal, was by this time a law lord and a member of the House of Lords. The story in which we young people used to revel included this passage of arms. Carson: 'What am I to think of a man who uses a friend as a ladder on which to climb to fame and then casts him away from beneath him? Such a man,' pointing dramatically to Birkenhead, sitting impassively on the Woolsack, 'I proscribe from my friendship for ever.'

Hansard does not give quite the same words but they certainly do not lack venom. 'I thought of the last thirty years, during which I was fighting with others whose friendship and comradeship I hope I will lose from tonight, because I do not value any friendship that is not founded upon confidence and trust. I was in earnest. What a fool I was. I was only a puppet, and so was Ulster, and so was Ireland, in the political game that was to get the Conservative Party into power. And of all the men in my experience that I think are the most loathsome it is those who will sell their friends for the purpose of conciliating their enemies, and, perhaps, worse still, the men who climb up a ladder into power of which even I may have been part of a humble rung, and then, when they have got into power, kick the ladder away without any concern for the pain, or injury, or mischief, or damage that they do to those who have helped them to gain power.'

When he came to reply, Birkenhead adopted a magnanimous tone. In the event the support for the Treaty was confirmed by 166 to 47 votes, although the latter total included some of the most respected peers, like Lord Salisbury. Birkenhead, in the story as told to us, had the last word. An attempt was made to reconcile these two old friends. They were put next to one another at a public dinner. Things were going well until Birkenhead said to Carson, 'You know, Ned, there was one thing you said about me which hurt.' Carson: 'What was that, F.E.?' Birkenhead: 'That bit about my using you as a ladder upon which to climb to fame.' Carson: 'But F.E., what's wrong with that?' Birkenhead: 'It was so damned true.'

Carson was in any case approaching the end of his career but the die-hard Tories did not easily forgive Birkenhead or the Coalition of which he was a member.

The Rhondda Peerage Case

Lord Birkenhead was involved in many controversial issues, legal and otherwise. One of the most complicated in terms of the arguments used on both sides but very simple in the outcome was the Rhondda Peerage Case. Few living peers would be aware – I myself was not until recently aware – that a woman, Lady Rhondda, came fairly close in 1922 to becoming a member of the House of Lords. In the event the first four women were admitted among the new Life Peers in 1958, 40 years after the first woman was elected to the House of Commons. The women hereditary peers were not admitted until five years later, as part of the measure which allowed peers to renounce their peerages.

On 6 March 1922 the Committee for Privileges, containing eight peers, three of them law lords – but under a lay Chairman of Committees – concluded in favour of Baroness Rhondda's application to become a member of the House of Lords. They pointed out that her father, Viscount Rhondda, had died on 3 July 1918 and that under his Patent Lady Rhondda succeeded to the title. 'But for the disqualification existing by reason of her sex the said Viscountess Rhondda would upon her succession to the said dignity have been entitled to receive a Writ of Summons to Parliament in right of the said dignity and to take her seat in Parliament accordingly.'

They went on to argue 'that the effect of the Sex Disqualification (Removal) Act, 1919, was to remove such disqualification, and that upon the passing of the said Act the said Viscountess Rhondda became entitled to receive a Writ of Summons to Parliament.'

When the report of the Committee was brought before the House of Lords it was violently resisted by the Lord Chancellor, Lord Birkenhead. He was well known to be opposed to the political emancipation of women generally. As he told the Lords during the debate on the Sex Disqualification (Removal) Bill in 1919 – the Government fortunately allowed a free vote on this clause – 'If we are to be abolished, I think that I would rather perish in the exclusive company of members of my own sex.' He laid much stress on the fact that the Committee for Privileges had not had the arguments against Lady Rhondda's position properly deployed by the Attorney-General, Sir Gordon Hewart. Hewart in fact had stated unequivocally that he agreed with the Committee in accepting Lady Rhondda's case. Birkenhead argued that representing the Crown he should at least have indicated the case against. Birkenhead persuaded the House of Lords, which probably needed little persuasion, to send the case back to the Committee of Privileges.

That Committee now wore a very different aspect: 26 members instead of eight with Birkenhead himself present and dominating the proceedings. This time, again not surprisingly, the Committee came down emphatically against Lady Rhondda. Birkenhead made a tremendous speech which is described by his biographer John Campbell, by no means an uncritical admirer, as a 'tour de force of intricate constitutional law'.

Ten law lords and twelve lay peers voted in the majority. Two law lords and two lay peers voted for Lady Rhondda. One of the dissenting Law Lords was Lord Haldane, formerly a Liberal and soon to become a Labour Lord Chancellor. I find it difficult to believe that legal considerations pointed clearly to one conclusion or the other. I admit to being entirely biased in favour of Lady Rhondda's application, both on general feminist grounds and as an intense admirer of the work of women peers since they came into the House. I cannot, however, avoid a sneaking sympathy with what was said by one of the lay peers, Lord Riddell: 'The Sex Disqualification (Removal) Act deals with juries, solicitors, students and teachers with meticulous care. Had the intention been to confer the important right now claimed surely Parliament would have inserted an express provision to that effect.'

It is just worth adding that the House of Commons had already indicated their desire to open the House of Lords to women. But the Lords, legal arguments apart, were resolutely opposed.

Trial by Peers

During this period an ancient privilege, if that is the right word, was made use of willy-nilly for the last time. Writing in 1894, Luke Owen Pike says this of the privilege of Trial by Peers: 'it has been a most jealously preserved of all the privileges of peers from the time of its establishment to the present. As between Sovereign and peers, and as between peers and peers, however, there is no doubt that every peer (including those of Scotland and of Ireland) has a right, when indicted of High Treason, of Felony, or of misprision if either, to be tried by peers.'

This deeply valued privilege however was for many centuries shrouded in ambiguity. The first real mention of the 'Judgement of Peers in England' occurred it seems in the Great Charter of King John (1215). 'No free man is to be taken, or imprisoned, or disseised or outlawed, or in any way destroyed nor will we proceed against him, or direct proceeding against him, except in accordance with the law of the land.' Pike insists that it would be impossible 'to exaggerate the importance of these provisions for the protection of the subject', but he insists also that they must be given a more restricted application than is usually given them. They must on no account be regarded as the equivalent of trial by jury which did not exist at that time. The judgement of peers had reference chiefly to the right of land-holders to their land, or to some matters connected with feudal tenure and its incidence. As time went on the significance of judgement by peers became clearer. Up till the end of the reign of Richard II there was not a very satisfactory system. In the first year of the reign of Henry IV, 1399, a statute was passed which effected a complete change in the law with regard to trial by peers. A great innovation was made by the institution of the Court of the Lord High Steward as a Court for the trial of peers by peers.

In 1900 Earl Russell was tried by 500 fellow peers for bigamy. He had been married in 1890 in England. In 1900 he obtained from a court in Nevada an order for divorce. He immediately went through a ceremony of marriage in Nevada. Three months later his first wife,

Countess Russell, obtained a decree for divorce on the grounds of his bigamous adultery. Earl Russell then found himself arrested and charged with bigamy. The Lord High Steward (the Lord Chancellor, Lord Halsbury) interpreted the relevant Act in such a fashion as to make Russell guilty of bigamy. 'On this ruling Russell pleaded guilty, his counsel addressed their Lordships on the mitigation of punishment, and Earl Russell himself was also allowed to make a speech.'

His sentence was three calendar months' imprisonment at Holloway as an offender of the First Division. It would appear that Russell served out his sentence of imprisonment, but later he got a free pardon from the King.

The Trial of Lord de Clifford 1935

Today this right of a peer to be, for a serious crime, tried by his peers, or indeed his disability to be tried otherwise, has been discontinued. It was brought to an end in 1948 but in 1935 it was still alive. On 15 August 1935 at 3 o'clock in the morning Lord de Clifford, the 26th Baron, his peerage going back to 1299, was involved in a road accident with a Mr Hopkins who unfortunately died as a result of the crash. Lord de Clifford was therefore tried for manslaughter and there was no way in which he could not be tried by his peers. In the event, 86 peers opted to serve on the tribunal, as compared with 500 when Lord Russell in 1901 was tried for bigamy. The proceedings were conducted with the utmost ceremony. The case has been brilliantly dealt with in a book by William Wells QC and a former MP.

One peculiar feature of the trial was that four High Court judges were called on to advise the House of Lords in reaching their conclusions although the peers sitting in judgement already included many leading judges of the day, the Lord Chancellor, the Lord Chief Justice and the Lords of Appeal in Ordinary. The trial itself was something of an anti-climax although the preliminary ritual is worth recalling. A few extracts are given below:

> The Lord Chancellor: My Lords, I move that the House do now adjourn into the Royal Gallery.
>
> On Question, Motion agreed to.
>
> The Officers, Attendants, and the Judges, Peers and Lords above set forth, with the Lord Privy Seal [Viscount Halifax], proceeded to the Royal Gallery, Garter King of Arms marshalling them in their due order.
>
> The Lords being come to the Royal Gallery were seated.
>
> The Lord Chancellor proceeded to his place, and the House was resumed.
>
> The Clerk of the Crown in Chancery, after making three reverences, presented the Commission under the Great Seal appointing the Lord High Steward on his knee to the Lord Chancellor, who delivered it back to him to read.
>
> The Clerk of the Crown made three reverences, and returned to the Table.
>
> The Serjeant-at-Arms: Oyez, oyez, oyez! Our Sovereign Lord the King strictly charges and commands all manner of persons to keep silence under pain of imprisonment.
>
> The Lord Chancellor: His Majesty's Commission is about to be read. Your lordships are desired to attend to it in the usual manner; and all others are likewise to stand up uncovered while the Commission is reading.
>
> All the Peers uncovered themselves, and they and all others stood up uncovered while the Commission was read.

The whole thing was in fact over quite quickly but not before Lord de Clifford was arraigned.

> Edward Southwell, Lord de Clifford, you as a Peer of England are indicted for manslaughter. The particulars of the offence are that you on the 15th day of August 1935 in the County of Surrey unlawfully killed Douglas George

Hopkins. You are also charged upon a Coroner's Inquisition with the manslaughter of Douglas George Hopkins. How say you, my Lord, are you Guilty of the Felony with which you are charged or Not Guilty?

Lord de Clifford: Not Guilty.

The Clerk of the Parliaments: How will you be tried?

Lord de Clifford: By God and my Peers.

The Clerk of the Parliaments: God send your Lordship a good deliverance. Serjeant-at-Arms, make proclamation.

The Attorney-General presented the case for the prosecution. Sir Henry Curtis Bennett replied for the defence. There was then an adjournment at the end of which the Lord Chancellor, described for this purpose as the Lord High Steward, announced that the question of law propounded had been submitted 'to His Majesty's judges who are here for the purpose of advising their Lordships' House upon questions of law which may arise during the course of the trial.' He went on: 'The Judges have unanimously advised their Lordships that your submission is well founded and that there is no case to answer. Their Lordships, in pursuance of that advice, have resolved to uphold your submission.' So that, in effect, was that. Nevertheless the Clerk of Parliaments called every peer by name beginning with a junior Baron and asked for their individual verdicts. One after another they replied: 'Not Guilty upon my honour.'

The Lord High Steward therefore pronounced that Edward Southwell, Lord de Clifford, was acquitted. The prisoner was brought to the Bar by the Yeoman Usher of the Black Rod, the Lord High Steward took leave of him with these kindly words: 'Edward Southwell, Lord de Clifford, you have been indicted for a felony, for which you have been tried by your Peers, and I have the satisfaction of declaring to you that their Lordships have pronounced you Not Guilty by a unanimous sentence.'

CHAPTER X

The House of Lords from 1945

It is impossible for the present writer, a member of the House of Lords from 1945, to treat the last 43 years in the House as objectively as the preceding 700. When the Labour Government came into power in 1945 its position in the House of Lords might appear to resemble that of the Liberals in 1906. But it was numerically very much weaker.

R. J. Minney, in his valuable *Life of Lord Addison*, points out that Addison, who had been leader of the Labour peers since 1940, had at his disposal a total of 16 supporters in a House of 831 voting members. He goes on to mention the fact that, when he assembled them for a preliminary talk, Addison was faced by only eight; illness or other work had kept half of them away.

Joining them myself at this time I regarded them with the deference due to the very old. Lord Listowel, Lord Faringdon, Lord Rothschild and Lord St. Davids were the only peers who belonged to my generation. I was just under 40 at the time. Until I read Mr Minney's book I forgot that Lord Passfield, better known as Sidney Webb, then aged 86, was one of us. He was by no means the only octogenarian. Now that I myself belong to that category their continued existence does not seem so peculiar.

Reinforcements have steadily arrived until there are at the time of writing more than 100 peers who take the Labour Whip, although it is not expected by the Whips that on any particular occasion more than two-thirds of the total could be relied on to pass through the Division Lobby.

By general agreement the relationship established between Lord Addison and Lord Salisbury was of crucial importance for the whole future of the House of Lords. Lord Addison died in 1951, having remained a vital influence not only in the House of Lords but in the councils of the Labour Cabinet until almost the end. He had been a Cabinet minister under Lloyd George as long ago as 1920. Before that, he had achieved much success as a Professor of Anatomy, giving his name to Addison's Disease, from which President Kennedy is supposed to have suffered. He was almost unbelievably fresh and vigorous for all his 76 years; he brought to bear a wealth of experience that no one in the House, even Lord Salisbury, could surpass.

I myself was very much his pupil. When I made my maiden speech I was under the impression that I was 'going strong'. Suddenly I was kicked on the back of the calf by Lord Addison. I looked round expecting some kind of embarrassment but was told instead, 'Take your hands out of your pockets.' On another occasion, I received the same physical correction, to be told this time (long before I intended to conclude): 'Sit down now. You've got the House with you. You'll lose them if you go on any longer.'

In an autobiography that I published in 1953 I describe my final visit to Lord Addison, desperately ill with cancer. 'You know, Frank,' he said smiling, 'I've had a lot of pain these last few months. At one moment I almost thought it was going to get me down.' A superb understatement indeed of what he had been and was still going through. I ended with lyrical words that I do not wish to retract. 'O valiant soul. Affectionate Nestor. Natural leader and never-to-be-forgotten teacher of men.'

Lord Salisbury, who did not die until 1972, confessed more than once his admiration for Addison and his conviction that the relationship between them was, as mentioned above, essential to the House of Lords in the next half century. The social atmosphere of complete equality and fraternity between the peers of all parties was established and has never been threatened. On one occasion a much-respected Labour backbencher caused high indignation among the Tory backbenchers by appearing to cast aspersions on their motives in regard to Rhodesia. Indeed, a number of them walked out muttering that these reflections on Lord Salisbury, who was not present, were quite out of keeping with the spirit of the House of Lords. Salisbury himself met the Labour peer in question and hastened to assure him that he was quite right to express his opinion if that was the way he felt. 'This is a House of Parliament, not a Club.' But he, in fact, more than anyone, has made sure that it has been a House of Parliament *and* a Club during all these years. I would suggest deliberately that it is the most unsnobbish Club in the world.

In practice all went smoothly for the first two years after the War. Addison himself was a very skilful debater. So in a different style was the Lord Chancellor, William Jowitt. William Jowitt once told me that the secret of advocacy is to find the worst thing that your opponent can say about your case and then say it yourself in your own way. Certainly, he was a master of that technique. I may be slightly, but not much, caricaturing his method when I recall his method of introducing a Bill unwelcome to the Conservatives. 'My Lords, I hate this Bill. I don't suppose that there is anyone in this House who dislikes it as much as I do. But, My Lords, have we any alternative? . . .' and so Bill after Bill was accepted by their Lordships.

There came a time, however, when the Government was faced with the fact that the House of Lords were extremely unlikely to accept the Bill for Nationalising Iron and Steel. Under the Parliament Act of 1911, it was impossible to be sure of carrying through any Bill resisted by the House of Lords in the fourth session. In 1947 the Government therefore introduced a New Parliament Bill in the House of Commons, a Bill dealing only with the powers of the House. There was a great outcry from both Conservatives and Liberals. The Lords adjourned while talks between the party leaders took place. The conference discussed powers and composition but broke down in April 1948 over the period of delay that the House of Lords should be able to impose on a Bill's progress.

It is noteworthy however that a tentative agreement had been reached on certain principles regarding the role and composition of a reformed House. It was agreed that a second Chamber should be 'complementary to and not a rival to the Lower House and that there should not be a permanent majority assured for any one political party, that heredity should not by itself constitute a qualification for admission to a reformed Second Chamber, and that women should be capable of being appointed Lords of Parliament.'

After the 1948 conference had broken down, the House of Lords rejected the Parliament Bill on Second Reading. The Bill was then passed into law in 1949 under the terms of the Parliament Act 1911, only the third Bill to be passed in this way. The Parliament Act 1949 amends its predecessor of 1911 by reducing the number of sessions in which a Bill must be passed by the Commons from three to two, and reducing the period between the first Second Reading and final passing in the Commons from two years to one.

The Act of 1949

I cannot remember much heat being engendered in the House over this Bill – surprisingly little, looking back. Lord Addison made the same point in introducing the Third Reading. 'Two years ago,' he said, 'when the Bill was first introduced it was denounced as a constitutional revolution. There were many forebodings as to what would happen, but' – he went on without, as far as I can recollect, any protest – 'there has been no uprising of public opinion about the Bill. The threatened stirring up of revolutionary feelings in the campaign against this Bill, and this is a reflection which I venture to make on what threatened two years ago – has fallen completely flat.' He paid obviously sincere tribute to what he called the high quality of our debates in the House. 'I am sure,' he went on, 'that people outside admire and respect the restraint of the noble Marquess, the Leader of the Opposition, on the conduct of our business.' He regretted Lord Salisbury's absence through indisposition. 'But the public are also aware that this House is overwhelmingly Conservative and that it has no representative authority.'

'It is not reasonable,' he went on, 'that this House should be able to sterilise two years out of the five years' work of another place.' In future the Conservative majority would admittedly be able to sterilise *one* year, but *two* was altogether too much of a bad thing.

Lord Swinton, a fine administrator and an eloquent polemical debater, took his stand where Conservative leaders have taken it on occasion for many years. He insisted on the right and duty of the House of Lords to make sure that the will of the people prevailed. 'Under our constitution, a government, possibly with a small majority, has unfettered power.' That power was unfettered 'except in so far as restraint may be exercised in case of need by a second chamber.' To weaken the restraining power of the Lords was to undermine democracy (my words, not his).

Lord Samuel, the Liberal leader, reminded us that he was the only survivor of the Asquith Cabinet that had carried the great Parliament Act of 1911. He felt, however, that that Act had worked extremely well and he considered that there was no need to alter it. When it came to the division the vote, as Addison had forecast, was to say the least unbalanced, Contents: 37; Not Contents: 110 (including Lord Samuel who in old age had graduated into the prize wit of the House).

It is worth noticing the references during this debate to the abortive attempt to reach an agreement about reform of the House. It seems to be accepted by all that agreement on the composition of the House had been substantially arrived at. Samuel felt that the responsibility for breakdown rested 'mainly with the Conservative Party'. 'They should,' he said, 'have agreed to the Government's proposal on the question of powers.' There was a difference of only three months in the period of delay between what they were willing to accept and what the Government proposed.

At first sight it may seem strange that the Government and the Conservative leaders came so close to an agreement on opposition. The truth was, of course, that the emergent House would not have been accepted as an ideal arrangement by the Labour leaders. So long as it contained an hereditary element it would remain suspect. It remained vital therefore for a Labour Government to be left with the power to enforce its legislation without what seemed to them unreasonable delay.

The Conservatives came back in 1951 and stayed in power for 13 years. Minor changes such as a provision for peers to obtain a leave of absence were effected. Reimbursement of expenses, very small at first but more realistic later, was introduced in 1957. A substantial reform came about in 1958. The Life Peerages Act of that year empowered the Crown to create life peers who would be entitled to sit and vote in the House of Lords and whose peerages would expire on their death. Just as significant was the fact that four of the initial life peerages were conferred upon women. Even so, the prejudice against their membership still excluded the considerable number of women with hereditary peerages.

The introduction of life peerages is generally regarded as having been of profound significance. I readily accept the fact that the numbers of the House would have increased unbearably if hereditary peerages had been created on the same scale. I have no idea, however, how many men and women have accepted life peerages who would have refused hereditary peerages. Personally I only know of four eminent persons since the war who are understood to have refused peerages of any kind: Sir Isaiah Berlin, Sir Kenneth Younger, Mr Robert Maxwell and Mr Jack Jones – unless we are to include Sir Winston Churchill. Sir Harold Macmillan accepted an hereditary peerage in the end.

The Peerage Act of 1963 was of almost equal significance. Mr Wedgwood Benn, heir to Lord Stansgate, had been campaigning for years for the right of peers to renounce hereditary peerages. He had his way at last in 1963, after a Joint Committee of both Houses had reported. Lord Home and Lord Hailsham were two of eleven peers who then or soon afterwards renounced their peerages. Both re-entered the House of Commons, in the process of standing for the leadership of their party, that is to say the premiership, Lord Home proving successful. They have since rejoined the House of Lords as life peers. The hereditary peerages have been kept alive for their offspring.

The women were at last to come in on the same footing as the men. There are now 67 of them. Baroness Young has been Leader of the House; Baroness Seear until recently the Leader of the Liberal Party. Baroness David is today Deputy Opposition Whip. I must at least mention current ministers like Baroness Trumpington and Baroness Hooper, and past ones like Baroness Serota, Baroness Birk and Baroness Phillips. The last-named was the first woman to be Lord Lieutenant of the County of London. Baroness Jeger was chairman of the Labour Party, Baroness Faithfull 'the mole of compassion' (my description) Director of Social Services for Oxford. The influence of women on social questions has been profound. I shall eagerly await the publication of *A Lady in the Lords* by Baroness Ewart-Biggs.

All Scottish peers, instead of a limited number of Scottish representative peers, are now admitted. Irish representative peers have by now died out. (No more Irish peers as such have been created.) In passing I might point out that Lord Listowel, the Lord Lucan of the time, and I myself have been among Irish peers entitled to sit in the House of Lords by virtue of an additional U.K. peerage. I myself was given an hereditary peerage as Lord Pakenham in 1945. In 1961, on the death of my brother, I inherited the title of Earl of Longford (Irish) and Lord Silchester (U.K.) I have been tempted to describe myself as the only peer at the present time who has been awarded a peerage and also inherited a seat in the House of Lords. This claim might be disputed by Lords Home and Hailsham who certainly inherited titles and after a period in the House of Commons were awarded life peerages. Occasionally, an hereditary peer is elevated in the peerage. Lords De Lisle and Rochdale are notable examples.

And so to 1964 when I became Leader of the House of Lords and a member of Harold Wilson's Cabinet. The strength of the Labour peers was much greater than in 1945, but in any showdown we would always be beaten by the Tory Opposition. In that sense, as in 1945, we existed and carried through our legislation on sufferance. On the other hand the Tories, under the very capable leadership of Lord Carrington, had their own problems. If they were seen to be making a nonsense of the House of Lords in Labour eyes and in the view of the majority of the population, they would bring about the abolition of their dearly loved House. Inevitably, therefore, they were in the position of being willing to wound and yet afraid to strike.

It was never absolutely clear to me what results Harold Wilson expected me to produce or hoped that I would produce. He was generous in congratulating me several times on the skilful way that I had steered legislation through the House, assisted by parliamentary colleagues of high class like Eddie Shackleton, Frank Beswick and Malcolm Shepherd, but I was never quite certain whether a showdown with the Lords giving the Government an excuse for drastic curtailment of their powers would not have suited him as well or better.

Be all that as it may, the Labour election manifesto for 1966 pledged the party, if returned to power, to introduce legislation 'to safeguard measures approved by the House of Commons from frustration by delay or defeat in the House of Lords'; in the event, a Labour administration under Mr Wilson was returned with a majority of 99.

I am not aware that up to that point there was any definite idea in the minds of the Labour Government about the steps necessary to reform the powers of composition of the Lords but here by an accident I intervened to play a part that might have been of great long-term significance but in the event came to nothing.

I was convinced, as any Labour Leader of the Lords must have been, that the House of Lords was full of anomalies and should be radically reformed. The idea of reducing the *powers* of the Lords had in one form or another been Labour policy for many years.

Abolition of the House had always had many supporters. What I was primarily concerned with, however, was to place the *composition* of the House of Lords on a rational footing. To quote something that I have written before, 'Such a project, one might think, would commend itself to all Liberals and Socialists, if it involved eliminating or at least much reducing the hereditary element. One might assume that large numbers of Conservatives would be opposed to reform for this very reason. In fact, the position was, from the beginning and throughout, much more complex.'

It will be recalled that as early as 1907 there had been a movement in high Conservative circles to reform the House of Lords to make it more defensible in the eyes of the public and thus to increase its influence. On the other hand the Labour Party were instinctively unwilling to do anything to bring about that result.

As it happens I came to the Leadership of the Lords with positive, and indeed dogmatic, ideas about the right way to reform the composition. From 1951 I had played golf at Rye every weekend with Henry Burrows, Clerk Assistant in the Lords (No. 2 at the Table). No weekend passed without our discussing Henry's special plan for reforming the House of Lords. 'The two-writ plan', as he called it. It very nearly, in a somewhat modified form, became the law of England.

Briefly, under the two-writ plan, all existing members of the House of Lords would continue to be allowed to come there and *speak*, but only those who were themselves created peers, either before or after the introduction of the scheme, would be allowed to *vote*. Hereditary peers as such would therefore lose the vote, although distinguished hereditary figures such as Lord Carrington and Lord Jellicoe on the Conservative side, or Lord Listowel or Lord Shepherd across the gangway, would obviously be given voting peerages and thus maintain their voting rights.

As things were, whoever had won the debate, the Conservatives triumphed in the voting lobby by virtue of the hereditary block. This domination would be broken with the disappearance of the hereditary peers as voters. From a democratic point of view, in the second half of the twentieth century, the main anachronism would disappear, which one might think (though one would be wrong) would appeal to all honest radicals. But matters initially did not work out that way at all.

A time came when I raised the whole issue of reforming the composition of the House of Lords in front of the Cabinet. Nothing could have been less successful. I was laughed to scorn. Gerald Gardiner, the Lord Chancellor, alone supported me. He had shared in producing a paper for the Cabinet. We dealt both with composition and with powers in which Gerald was distinctly more interested. Harold Wilson disposed of our item with the words, 'I can imagine nothing quite so divisive as an attempt to reform the House of Lords.' There was cordial agreement with him. My angry protests were not taken too seriously. Dick Crossman in his diaries has indicated his own frivolous reception of my reform proposals.

But at this point the cause of Lords reform had a lucky break. In the autumn of 1966 Dick Crossman became Leader of the House of Commons. He was quick to realise that it was impossible to make sense of the House of Commons while leaving the House of Lords fundamentally anomalous. He became converted in principle to something like the two-writ plan for the Lords. From that moment onwards its chances of success rose markedly. He became the most significant force in favour of reform. It is still not clear to me at what point Lord Carrington, leader of the Opposition in the House of Lords, began to work for Lords reform. At any rate it was not long before we were in touch and clearly thinking along similar lines.

I brought Peter Carrington and Dick Crossman together at dinner. At the beginning of 1967 Eddie Shackleton became Deputy Leader of the House of Lords. His great friend George Jellicoe and of course Gerald Gardiner, the Lord Chancellor, made up a group of peers who, cutting across party lines, brought the reform of the composition of the House of Lords to within an ace of success. But it was not to be. The Queen's Speech for 1967/68 contained the following words: 'Legislation will be introduced to reduce the powers of the House of Lords and to eliminate its present hereditary basis, thereby enabling it to develop within the framework of a modern Parliamentary system. My Government are prepared to enter into consultations appropriate to a constitutional change of such importance.'

Inter-party talks on Lords reform took place at a conference from 8 November 1967 to 20 June 1968. In January 1968 I resigned from the leadership of the Lords and the Cabinet on an issue of educational principle. The really hard work was done after my departure by those mentioned above, especially Eddie Shackleton. The talks were broken off by the government in June 1968 because the Southern Rhodesia (United Nations Sanctions) Order (1968) was rejected by the Lords at the suggestion of the Conservative Opposition leadership in that House. Substantial agreement had been reached by this time between the parties on proposals for a comprehensive reform of both the composition and the powers of the House of Lords.

The Government decided to proceed with a scheme on the lines worked out in conference. It published in November 1968 a White Paper 'House of Lords Reform' which reflected in all essential details the outcome of the talks. The White Paper was debated in both Houses. In the Lords opinion was generally favourable. It was approved by 261 votes to 56. In the Commons, the two front benches were united in support of the measure, but there was much criticism from the backbenchers who were overwhelmingly hostile.

The Government went ahead with the Bill. On a Government two line whip and a free vote by the Conservative and Liberal Parties the Bill received a Second Reading in the Commons on 3 February 1969. But it was always in trouble at the Committee stage. A strange combination, led by my then son-in-law Hugh Fraser, of whom I was very fond, and Enoch Powell on the one side, and Michael Foot on the other fought a long delaying action. After the House had spent eleven days in Committee with little progress made, the Prime Minister announced the abandonment of the Bill on 17 April 1969, two and a half years after I had originally raised the matter with the Cabinet. The House of Commons did not wish to see a House of Lords with a rational composition, a rival to itself in influence with the public.

Janet Morgan

A very valuable assessment of the role of the House of Lords since the war is that of Janet Morgan (*The House of Lords and the Labour Government 1964–1970*). In particular she gives a penetrating description of the attitude of the House of Lords to the Southern Rhodesia (United Nations Sanctions) Order (1968) and the Redistribution of Seats Bill (1969). The Southern Rhodesian Order (1968) provides the one serious occasion since the war when the House of Lords appeared to be squaring up to the Commons. The Commons first discussed and passed the Order on 17 June 1968. On that and the following day it was debated in the House of Lords.

The 'Rhodesia Lobby' led by Lord Salisbury, whose prestige, once unparalleled, was still very high among Conservative backbenchers, opposed the Order from the beginning. As Janet Morgan points out, the whole question of the Lords' powers in relation to delegated legislation was a delicate one. Orders unlike Acts are not subject to the provisions of the Parliament Act. Nevertheless Lord Carrington, aware of every nuance in the situation, psychological and constitutional, admitted 'it would be unusual, more it would be unprecedented I believe, for your Lordships to reject this Order'. But he continued: 'It is equally clear that this House would be within its constitutional rights in so doing, and thus affording to public opinion, to the Government, and if you wish, to the Opposition as well, a period for reflection. After all, that is what a Second Chamber is for.'

There is every reason to suppose that Lord Carrington himself was not in favour of rejecting the Order. The pressures on him however from his own back benches led by his former Leader, Lord Salisbury, were overwhelming. He had shown himself capable of resisting such pressures on more than one occasion but this time, so it seems, he felt compelled to go along with the stream. At any rate a debate of much intensity followed. Fifty-one speeches were made on 17 and 18 June, 26 broadly in favour of the Order and 25 against. When the House divided 184 peers voted Content and 193 Not Content. In retrospect, considering the lead which was ultimately given by the Conservative Ministers, the majority against the measure was extraordinarily small. An analysis of the vote is worth putting on record. It is well set out by Janet Morgan:

> It is interesting that the vote was lost so very narrowly. The Labour Whips were gratified to find that the Contents were made up of 84 Labour Peers, supported by 18 Bishops, 23 Liberals, 1 Communist, 50 crossbenchers, and 8 Conservatives. As the number of Labour Peers among the working House was anyway only 95 ... this was an impressive showing.

The 193 Not Content were all Conservatives except for 15 crossbenchers. This unusual predominance of cross-bench peers of one side or the other was very nearly decisive.

The story of the 'Seats Bill' does not make happy reading for Labour supporters. In 1969 the Home Secretary was statutorily required to lay before both Houses of Parliament Orders giving effect to the last report of the Parliamentary Boundary Commission. It was commonly agreed that the findings of the Commission would be unfavourable to the Labour Party. The Conservatives naturally demanded that the Orders should be laid forthwith. The Labour Party tried to find an excuse for delay. The Bill when it reached the Lords was given a Second Reading without a Division but at the Committee stage a crucial amendment was carried 270 to 96 against the Government. Of the 96 peers supporting the Government, 93 took the Whip. No bishop supported the Government. This must be regarded as an occasion when the Government had no support outside their own 'tied following'. In the event, the House of Commons brought back the Southern Rhodesia Order without further resistance from the Lords. They avoided the issue presented by the Redistribution of Seats Bill by a tactical device. When the Conservatives came in to office in 1970 they put the recommendations of the Boundary Commission into force.

Janet Morgan considered that the attitude of the Conservative peers in regard to the Seats Bill presented them at their best in sharp contradistinction to their attitude over the Southern Rhodesia Order. It indeed provided them with their finest hour. More broadly she takes a very favourable view of the behaviour of the Lords during these years. 'The Lords,' she says in conclusion, 'in workman-like fashion are adapting to their Parliamentary and public circumstances and treading carefully. In 1974 as in 1964 . . . the Lords have continued to alter their procedures and the scope of their activities at a discreet and even pace. Their survival in the face of sustained and varied pressures suggests, not bemused detachment, but an evolutionary resilience of which Darwin himself would have approved.' Two or three years later we shall find the Labour Party much less happy about the behaviour of their Lordships.

CHAPTER XI

The House of Lords Today

I must reproduce figures given at the beginning of this book about the relative strengths of the various parties in the House of Lords. The figures for December 1986 were as follows:

Conservative	417
Independent (Cross Bench)	245
Labour	118
Liberal	42
Social Democrat	43

Do these figures guarantee the Conservatives an automatic victory in the House of Lords? No simple answer should be attempted. An Information Sheet issued by the Journal and Information Office, House of Lords, for December 1986 put the matter this way: 'The 1968 White Paper stated that "the Conservatives have always in modern times been able to command a majority". In recent years this has not been the case. During the Heath administration (1970–4) there were 26 Government defeats. The total number of defeats since the 1979 election passed 100 in October 1986; the first Thatcher administration (1979–83) sustained 45 defeats, the second (1983–7) sustained 62 in its first three sessions.'

How could the Opposition achieve these results when the Conservatives have nominally at least 300 more members than the Labour Party?

An important clue is to be found on page 27 of the report by the Group on the Working of the House, July 1987 under the chairmanship of Lord Aberdare, Chairman of Committees.

COMPOSITION OF THE HOUSE
WORKING HOUSE*: BREAKDOWN BY PARTY

Party	Period			
	1967–68	1983–84	1984–85	1985–86
Conservative	125	167	170	168
By Succession	87	100	106	101
Created	38	67	64	67
Labour	95	98	91	88
By Succession	14	7	8	7
Created	81	91	83	81
Liberal	19	25	26	27
By Succession	11	9	12	12
Created	8	16	14	15
S.D.P.	N/A	21	23	24
By Succession		5	6	7
Created		16	17	17
Independent	52	76	74	73
By Succession	26	33	34	36
Created	26	43	40	37
i) Cross Bench	N/A	67	66	70
By Succession		33	32	36
Created		34	34	34
ii) Unspecified	N/A	9	8	3
By Succession		0	2	0
Created		9	6	3
*Total**	291	387	384	380
By Succession	138	154	166	163
Created	153	233	218	217

* For the purposes of this table the 'working House' has been taken to be those peers who attended at least one-third of the Sittings of the House.

176

On this sort of calculation the Conservatives, with 168 active peers, would outnumber, but not by an overwhelming majority, the Labour and Alliance peers together (168 against 139). The Independents with 73 on paper hold the balance but three-quarters of them would have to vote against the Conservatives before the latter could be defeated.

This kind of scenario is not very common. During the last ten years of Conservative government a clear majority of the Independents can be looked on as likely to support that government either because it is the government of the day or because they are conservative-minded. The Government Chief Whip, in these latter days the exceptionally discerning Lord Denham, can never however be sure of this happening on any particular occasion. To quote his words, 'In point of fact government defeats always consist of occasions when all the other three parties plus well over half the Independents present vote against the government.'

I must record another assessment. Lady Hylton-Foster, who presides with such unobtrusive skill over the Independents, and is modestly described as their Convenor, considers that the Independent peers divide fairly evenly on a division between Government and Opposition when it actually comes to a vote. I do not however find that this view is widely shared.

One must be careful in any case not to underestimate the influence of the cross-bench peers. They speak with much authority on their own subjects without any party political bias. If there is very strong feeling the majority may vote one way. The Government of the day seems to be very much alive to the danger of a majority of cross-bench peers being opposed to or in favour of an amendment. In such circumstances in order to avoid going to a vote they often undertake to have another look at the position.

Elsewhere I have tried to sum up the influence of the bishops in the House of Lords. In the last few years they have expressed many reservations about the trend of Government social and economic policies. But probably not two peers would agree on what their influence amounts to at the present time. I like to believe that nearly all peers would welcome their spiritual presence.

When the Opposition has won a Division, the most obvious factor at work has been a combination between the Labour Party, the Liberals and the SDP but the attitude of the Conservative peers has been equally crucial. No one, perhaps even their own leaders, can estimate how far their absence from the Government Division lobby is due to inability to attend the House or how far to a conscientious reluctance to vote for the measure in question. Statistically the numbers of votes cast by Conservative peers against the Government has never been large. But a number of such peers have revealed an independence of spirit whose total influence is beyond calculation. Lord Molson (an oratorical hero of mine from Oxford days), Lord Selkirk (a younger son who uniquely inherited a title), Lady Faithfull, and the Duke of Norfolk, the senior Catholic, come easily to mind. We come back to the basic fact of the House of Lords being a chamber with a large Conservative majority but just as palpably a part-time institution. I would add, incidentally as regards the latter attribute, all the better for that.

It is difficult, indeed impossible, to measure at all precisely the impact of the Opposition in the House of Lords. The number of Government defeats is only part of the story. 'I have always myself held the view,' Lord Denham tells me, 'that amendments to a Bill won by argument on the floor of the House as against those won by a vote in the division lobby are on a ratio of something like 10 to 1, though I have no statistics to prove this.'

From the Government's point of view, time is of the essence. They are not infrequently ready to reach an accommodation with the Lords in order to avoid delay. Only occasionally has the House of Lords overly insisted on an amendment that has been passed in their House but disagreed to in the House of Commons. In recent years when such a situation seemed likely to arise, it has been the House of Commons that has bowed to the will of the House of Lords, often because of pressure of time.

The following figures relating to the session 1985/86 may be of interest. In that session 12 of the 19 amendments made in the Lords following a Government defeat survived substantially intact. In a further four cases the Government came some way to meet a point carried on a division by the Opposition without making it in full. In only three cases out of the 19 did the Government reverse an amendment carried against them in the Lords on a division without making any concessions.

After 43 years in the House, I am aware that in the last resort the Conservative Party, in or out of office, can prevail in nine cases out of ten – that is until the measure goes to the House of Commons, where all sorts of things may happen. But that phrase 'in the last resort' covers many possibilities. In the first place, the Conservative leaders in the House are well aware that they must not seem to be abusing their power. They might well meet with retribution at the hands of the public. But secondly a vast number of issues arise today which are not party questions. The government of the day has the task of making the initial proposals, but they are frequently ready to make many concessions in the light of discussion. There are only a limited number of occasions where it is vital to their programme to make a stand.

The report by a group under the chairmanship of Lord Aberdare, Chairman of Committees, laid stress on the increased daily attendance of peers. The large expansion of life peers, now numbering 346, had been in their eyes of the utmost significance. 'Following the report of 1971,' they observe, 'many of the Life Peers are ex-MPs or from local government, and approach their role as members of the House of Lords with a spirit of professionalism which was largely unfamiliar to the House prior to the passage of the Life Peerages Act, 1958.'

It would be disingenuous not to mention the effect of the reimbursement allowances (which did not begin to exist until 1957) in encouraging the attendance and professionalism of members. Be that as it may, the House of Lords today provides the widest selection of views and expert knowledge that can be found in any legislature I am aware of. I have said that in the last resort, the Conservative Party can prevail in the House of Lords. In the last resort, the government of the day if they enjoy a majority in the Commons can get their measures through under the Parliament Acts if their programme seems to be at stake.

That statement is subject to one reservation. In the last session of a parliament the Lords have it in their power to hold up a measure pending an election – a point of more obvious relevance during a

Labour than a Conservative government. But what has just been written might give a false impression of the contemporary House of Lords. Most members of the House are not preoccupied with the party dogfight. They are accustomed to work within a well-understood framework of party government, but nearly all of them have other causes at heart.

The Labour Party in the House of Lords

The Labour Party, coming into office for a short while in the 1920s, did not achieve real power until 1945. It represented a new element of the first importance in the history of the House of Lords. The House of Lords, traditionally conceived as a bastion of conservatism, had never been likely to appeal to devout socialists. The Labour Party attack has been two-fold: firstly in its ideological objections, not to a Second Chamber as such, but to a Second Chamber based on the hereditary principle; secondly, its practical, party-political objection to the House of Lords having an overwhelmingly built-in Conservative majority.

It cannot be said, however, that the Labour Party in the half-century after 1935 has paid much attention to the House of Lords. Between the 1930s and the late 1960s the Labour Party Conference passed no resolution on the House of Lords, although until 1935 the Labour Party Manifesto had quite often committed the Party to abolition, and Attlee at the beginning of the election in 1945 said, 'We give clear notice that we will not tolerate obstruction of the people's will by the House of Lords.' But the abolition of the Lords was in no sense an issue during the next 30 years.

But as the House of Lords seemed to be making more and more a nuisance of itself during the 1974–79 Labour government, the abolition of the Lords came back on to the Labour agenda. A fundamental reappraisal was carried out in 1976 which led to a comprehensive statement by the National Executive of the Labour

Party. This was approved that autumn by the Party Conference. The conclusion of the 1977 document must be quoted verbatim:

> We believe that Labour's next Manifesto should contain a commitment to introduce legislation at an early stage in the new Parliament, and should include a passage along the following lines:
> 'Should we become the Government after the next General Election, we intend to abolish the House of Lords. No doubt given such an electoral mandate, the Lords would agree to this, but should they not, we would be prepared to use the Parliament Acts or advise the Queen to use her prerogative powers to ensure this. Unless something else were done, this would remove the Lords' complete veto on an extension of the life of a House of Commons beyond five years. To safeguard the electors' rights, therefore, we propose that such extension should be subject to approval by a referendum or, in time of war, by a two-thirds majority of the House of Commons.'

At the beginning of the 1980s, as doubts began to be expressed within the Executive about the practicality of Lords abolition, there were on the face of it only two ways of bringing this about: the first was to abolish the Lords under the Parliament Act which involved a delay of little more than a year, the second to obtain sufficient peerages or promises of peerages from the Crown to overwhelm the Conservative resistance. There was sufficient doubt in the minds of the leadership about the legality of the first method to discourage recourse to it. Nor did the option of creating 500 or more peers, as Asquith threatened to do in 1911, seem more attractive.

The more the National Executive of the Party investigated the steps required, the more their doubt increased. There was nevertheless no intention whatever of allowing the Lords to thwart the next Labour government.

The 1983 Election Manifesto contained this passage: 'Take action to abolish the undemocratic House of Lords as quickly as possible and, as an interim measure, introduce a Bill in the first session of parliament to remove its legislative powers – with the exception of those which relate to the life of a parliament.'

But in 1987 there was silence in the Election Manifesto for the first time. Are we to conclude that the spirited criticism of government measures under the Conservatives and the 100 Government defeats had produced in the mind of the Labour Party a dawning consciousness that the House of Lords might not be such a bad thing after all? The possibility had occurred to most of the Labour members of the House a good deal earlier.

The Conservative approach to the future of the House of Lords

In March 1978, a Conservative review committee published a contribution to the discussion. It was an exceptionally strong committee under the chairmanship of Lord Home, a former Prime Minister, Lord Blake, the leading Conservative historian of the day, Baroness Young, for some years Leader of the House of Lords, Mr Kenneth Baker MP, at the time of writing involved in the largest educational reforms of the century and, to quote one of Winston Churchill's phrases, 'other paladins'.

The committee say plainly that they wish to halt and indeed reverse 'the drift towards a unicameral form of parliamentary government'. They express the fear that 'the present House of Lords faces gradual but relentless atrophy; at worst it may be swept away by government impatient of the modest checks it imposes on the passage of legislation.'

'The case,' they say, 'for radical reform of the House of Lords is thus effectively the case for stronger constitutional safeguards.' They continue, 'In such a situation only a second chamber with very strong moral authority could be expected to provide an effective constitutional check. In the present climate of opinion that moral authority could only come from the direct election of its members.'

They canvass the various matters of election and face the recognised difficulties. They believe that the best hope of constructive reform is a hybrid; a second chamber constituted on a combined basis of election and nomination. They are thoroughly sophisticated in recognising again the difficulties involved in such proposals. Finally they suggest a new total membership of 400: 60% of these would be elected directly or indirectly; 40%, or 160, would be recruited from the present House of Lords membership.

Every possible argument for or against their own proposal is discussed at considerable length. Their conclusion should be carefully noted. The merit, they say, of this particular scheme of a mixed composition is that it seeks to combine the enhanced legitimacy and hence more defensible composition of a directly elected House with an element of continuity with the historic House of Lords. This was once described by Lord Bryce in a famous report as 'the oldest and most venerable of all British institutions, reaching back beyond the Norman Conquest and beyond King Alfred into the shadowy regions of Teutonic antiquity.' I doubt whether many historical scholars would trace the origins of the present House so far back. I do not dare to quarrel with the submission of this high level Conservative committee that the hybrid solution they recommend would be acceptable to Conservative opinion. On the other hand it is never likely to be accepted by the Labour Party or, I should imagine, any party left of centre, as a final solution.

The Paving Bill

The story of what is usually called Paving Bill 1984 is worth spelling out. A Conservative government was defeated in the House of Lords on a significant issue and forced to change its mind. They had as previously mentioned been defeated more than 100 times since 1979. But no defeat meant as much at the time as that on the Paving Bill. They may have afterwards been quite glad to have been forced

183

to abandon an untenable position. But at the time there was no doubt about their mortification. The so-called Paving Bill represented an attempt to prevent the local election due to take place in May 1985 going forward while the Bill to abolish the Greater London Council and the Metropolitan Councils was still under parliamentary discussion.

In a sense the Government achieved their purpose, but not at all in the way intended. They were taken to task by the House of Lords collectively for what was widely regarded as an unsavoury manoeuvre. The most crucial of the debates took place on 28 June 1984. *The Government plan was to abolish the existing local authorities as soon as a Second Reading of the Bill had been passed by the House of Commons.* Pending new arrangements the gap would be filled by temporary bodies elected by the Borough and District Councils. Lord Elwyn-Jones, the former Labour Lord Chancellor, introduced an amendment which he was fully entitled to call All-Party. His amendment ran as follows: 'Parts I and II of this Act shall not come into force until a decision has been taken by Parliament on the continued existence of the Greater London Council and Metropolitan Councils and such decision shall not be deemed to have taken place until Royal Assent has been given to an Act dealing with those matters.'

He explained that the aim of the first amendment was to ensure that no elections took place unless and until Parliament, that is until both Houses of Parliament, decided what was to take the place of the existing Councils. He laid supreme stress, as other speakers did later, on the fact that *both* Houses of Parliament must reach a decision before the local elections were cancelled. Under the Government's scheme they would be cancelled after the Second Reading in one House, the Commons, of a Bill abolishing the GLC. Lord Elwyn-Jones stuck to the constitutional rather than the administrative or political arguments.

'I want to make it clear at the outset that, in considering Amendment No. 1, we are not debating in the slightest degree whether the present GLC is a good GLC or whether the six county councils are admirable or bad county councils. That is not the issue which we are discussing. On this amendment we are not discussing whether any of those councils deserve to be abolished or what merits would arise from that.' What he was saying was, though he did not use this word, that the Government's scheme would be treating with contempt the House of Lords and, to a lesser extent, the House of Commons. What he actually said was:

'What the Government are trying to do is rendering a great disservice to Parliament, and this at a time when parliamentary institutions are losing the certainty they once had, and fears are growing that the House of Commons and the House of Lords are becoming ciphers and that political power has wholly passed into the hands of the Executive.' It was one of the best of his many good speeches.

The next speech, however, was in the circumstances even more notable. It came from Lord Molson, a former Conservative minister. He spoke just as strongly as Lord Elwyn-Jones against the Bill in its present form. He indicated that when the main Bill to abolish the Greater London Council and the Metropolitan County Councils came before the House he would vote for the Second Reading. (He did so in the event but took a sharply critical line in Committee.) 'The trouble, however,' he said, 'which arises out of this Paving Bill is that it authorises the abolition of the Councils before we have decided what to put in their place. It is in fact a case of putting the cart before the horse.' That might have been regarded as an administrative argument but his criticism went deeper.

'I regard it,' he said, 'as an unprecedented and unconstitutional procedure for this Bill to come into operation to abolish democratic elections due to take place in May 1985 simply on the passing of the Second Reading in another place of the main Bill. The legislature of this realm is the Queen-in-Parliament, and this Bill should only come into operation, as this amendment provides, after the main Bill has passed all its stages in both Houses and receives the Royal Assent.'

The debate which followed was bound to be one-sided. The unfortunate minister, Lord Bellwin, respected in the House for his first-hand knowledge of local government, had what was generally considered an impossible task. He argued in effect that it was impossible for the main Bill to make its way into law before the local elections of 1985. It was only commonsense therefore to cancel those elections which would rapidly be nullified. He reminded the House that local elections had been cancelled before in anticipation of a major reorganisation of local authorities, in 1963 and 1972, for example. But when it came to the vote the Government was well and truly defeated: 191 voted for the amendment, only 143 for the government. It was a remarkable victory – or defeat, according to the way one looked at it.

That was on 28 June. On 23 July the Bill was passed through its final stages, but it was a very different Bill. Lord Bellwin admitted in moving that the Bill do pass that, 'The Bill as it now stands is somewhat different from that which was presented here on May 24th. This reflects the operation of Your Lordships' will and the Government's response', in other words the Government's concession to their defeat. He insisted however: 'The Bill's essential purpose remains the same.' That is not exactly how most members of the House saw the change. The Bill now proposed that the present members of the GLC and the Metropolitan County Councils should continue in office until abolition. He could fairly claim that as originally claimed the local elections in question would be cancelled pending a decision by both Houses of Parliament on the Bill. But the all important change was that the local authorities in question would not be abolished. They would remain in existence until both Houses of Parliament had reached a decision on the main Bill. Whatever the administrative implications the constitutional proprieties, above all the constitutional position of the House of Lords, would be preserved.

The Local Government Bill 1985 (Abolition of the GLC and Metropolitan Councils)

The debates on this Bill epitomise the situation and role of the House of Lords in the 1980s. The Bill was bitterly opposed by the

Opposition parties and plenty of others. The Government prevailed in the sense that the Bill was eventually passed with relatively few changes but the debates were hard fought and of high quality both emotionally and intellectually.

Out of the many and prolonged debates I must concentrate on a few happenings. On 15 April 1985 the Minister of State, Department of the Environment, Lord Elton, rose to move that the Bill be read a second time. His peroration sums up a speech which was all the more remarkable because he had been drafted in at the last minute owing to the illness, fatal as it proved, of Lord Avon.

'I shall tell your Lordships just this,' concluded Lord Elton, 'this Bill rests four-square upon long experience of a system that is inefficient and keeps important decisions at a distance from the people. It rests four-square upon an election pledge in a programme approved by the British electorate. It will save money. It will give electors a closer interest in local government affairs. It deserves your support.'

By 1985 the Labour Party in the Lords had come to accept the convention, established decades previously, that they did not oppose Bills on Second Reading which had been passed by the House of Commons. All the more so if the proposal had been contained in the manifesto of the government party. Baroness Birk, leading for the Opposition, moved however an amendment which went as close to rejection as was compatible with the convention. Baroness Birk's amendment read: 'This House regrets the failure to provide a local and democratic framework for the strategic services essential to the capital city and the metropolitan areas.'

Some twelve hours later, after more than 50 speeches had been delivered, she rose to wind up the debate. She felt entitled to make the claim that, 'The weight of expressed opinion in nearly every speech has been highly critical of various aspects of the Bill as it now stands.'

Special interest attached to the speech of Lord Plummer who had from 1967 to 1973 been leader of the Conservative majority in the GLC. Nothing could have been blunter than his language: 'Like others who have spoken, I believe this Bill to be hastily assembled, badly thought out and unlikely to meet the needs of the huge populations which it will affect.' And again at the end of his speech: 'The Bill as it is now written will not meet the needs and expectations of Londoners. I earnestly hope that amendments will be carried.'

On 26 April the *Guardian* reported: 'Senior Cabinet Ministers were last night striving to avert a Tory revolt in the House of Lords next week which could ensure the survival of an elected authority for London.'

There was a genuine trial of strength on 30 April. In this case an amendment was moved by the Independent peer, Lord Hayter, supported on the Order Paper by Lord Plummer, Lady Faithfull, and Lord Seebohm, an independent expert on social questions. The amendment began: 'On the abolition date there shall be established a body corporate known as the London Metropolitan Authority' and it continued, 'The London Metropolitan Authority shall consist of members elected by the local government electors of Greater London in accordance with this Act and the Representation of the People Act 1983. As from the abolition date the London Metropolitan Authority established by this section shall be the strategic authority for Greater London. The London Metropolitan Authority shall only exercise such functions as are vested in it under this Act and shall do so within the financial provision laid down under this Act.'

The division, when it came, was perhaps the most crucial of any that took place, if only because the proposed amendment went so close to the heart of the proposed arrangements. In the event the Government prevailed by just four votes – 213 to 209. The *Daily Telegraph* reported, 'The Government narrowly avoided a knock-out blow in the Lords last night over its plans to scrap the GLC and the Metropolitan Counties. A wafer-thin majority of only four votes saved the Bill from being wrecked but left it in deep trouble for the coming weeks.' The report went on later, 'The four-vote majority was due to the arrival of many Tory Lords who rarely visit the House. One peer said, "The Whips were dragging them in on stretchers".'

On 7 May the Government were twice beaten, by 152 to 135 and 117 to 103. On the first occasion the amendment ran: 'The

Secretary of State shall before the abolition date lay before Parliament a report on the steps he will take to secure the full adoption by metropolitan district councils and the London borough councils of those facilities, services, and responsibilities for the protection and enjoyment of the countryside which serve the continuing needs of the wider country areas and neighbouring populations.'

On the second occasion the proposal carried was of high importance. The following clause was to be inserted:

Highway and Road Traffic Functions

The Secretary of State shall by order taking effect on the abolition date make provision for the London Residuary Body to exercise the following functions relating to highways and road traffic in London to the extent and in the manner that such order shall provide:

(a) that the Body shall have a duty to prepare, in consultation with the borough councils, plans relating to highways and traffic in Greater London and the Body and borough councils shall have regard to such plans when exercising their statutory functions.

And the proposal was spelt out in detail.

To quote the *Daily Telegraph* again: 'Two defeats spelled trouble for the Government in the Lords last night when peers imposed major changes during committee-discussion on the Local Government Bill. There were majorities of 17 and 14 against the Government. The first vote resulted from environmental worries over the future of Green Belt land. The second, more seriously, wrote in provisions to create strategic highway authorities for London and six metropolitan county areas with the demise of the GLC and other metropolitan councils.'

On 9 May and 13 May the Government suffered further defeats by four votes and eleven votes (170 to 166 and 142 to 133). On the first occasion an amendment was passed which would open the way for establishing corporate waste disposal authorities for Greater London and the six Metropolitan Councils. On the second occasion an amendment introduced by the Bishop of London interfered with ministers' contingency plans for possible future dismemberment of the Inner London Education Authority. On 20 May a further Government defeat was staved off by a series of undertakings about the future of voluntary organisations.

The Bill was duly carried and sent back to the Commons with amendment on 2 July. For our purposes a particular argument submitted by Lord Elton should be recorded.

Lord Elton, supporting a statement made on 26 April in the House by the Chief Whip Lord Denham insisted that 'In almost every case and in almost every way of looking at it, the Government do not have an overall majority in this House.' He repeated the statement with emphasis: 'We are not operating with a built-in majority my Lords, we have to persuade your Lordships and that is the result which your Lordships see in the Division Lobby.' Lord Elton argued that what he called a number of resounding defeats of Her Majesty's Government was a further proof that there was not this built-in majority. On this particular Bill he pointed out, 'We have voted I believe 30 times and we are sending to another place over 90 amendments. So if your Lordships are in doubt as to whether or not this is a revising chamber that doubt may be set at rest.'

The struggle ended for the time being at any rate with a fairly conciliatory statement by the minister Patrick Jenkin in the House of Commons. He urged MPs to reject the Lords' amendments which provided for joint London and countryside authorities to deal with highways and road traffic and with waste disposal. 'This,' commented the *Financial Times* on 9 July, 'was the only departure from the otherwise conciliatory tone of a speech in which he urged MPs to accept the bulk of the Lords' amendments subject to minor drafting changes.'

CHAPTER XII

Some Social Concerns

There has been one striking feature of the House of Lords since the war which is without parallel in the 700 years of its history. It has taken an initiative (or at any rate endorsed by a majority, a distinctive position) on a number of social questions, more or less irrespective of party. The immense increase in the number of independent peers has brought a wealth of distinction and expertise which was previously lacking in the social area.

The House has since the war revealed a stronger Christian component than the Commons. It is not difficult to see why this should have been so. We have started off after all with 26 bishops, which is 26 more than they have.

In another book (*The Bishops*) I have attempted to assess their contribution. Here I will say only that they enrich every debate which their diocesan duties enable them to attend. In recent years, leading non-conformist divines like Lord Soper and Lord Macleod have strengthened greatly the religious front. The names of many laymen spring to mind. Lord Halsbury, Lord Ingleby and Lord Robertson have played leading parts in the House of Lords but they would not, I imagine, have sought election to the House of Commons. Lord Nugent, who has been an immensely effective spokesman for Christianity in the House of Lords in recent years, was admittedly a minister in the Commons but he seems to have found much more scope in our House. The present Duke of Norfolk has proved a popular, astute and humorous leader of the Catholic peers. On one occasion he mobilised ecumenical and all-party support to defeat the Government on an issue of local 'bussing'.

Until 1947 the Catholic peers were placed in italics in Vacher's Parliamentary Companion. From 1833, when that Companion was inaugurated, Catholic peers were marked out in this kind of way. It was only four years since Catholic emancipation in 1829. One must assume that anti-Catholic feeling was still powerful. It would be difficult to detect signs of it today but of course a Catholic may not be the best judge!

It would be wrong to ignore the presence among us of a number of dedicated non-Christian humanists. Their moment of glory was the passage of the Abortion Law Reform Act 1967 (see below).

The topics which I will select for brief discussion are capital punishment (from 1956), homosexual law reform (from the same year), abortion law reform (from 1966), the disabled (from 1970) and pornography and connected matters (from 1971).

Capital Punishment

In the case of capital punishment the majority of the House of Lords took a long time to come into line with the House of Commons, clinging defiantly to the death penalty. On homosexuality they led the way. On abortion they led the way again, I would think disastrously, though there have lately been signs of what I would call better things in both Houses. On pornography, the stance of the Lords has been on the whole bolder than that of the Commons. On the disabled, the historic initiative came from Alfred Morris in the House of Commons. But the Lords have strenuously followed it up over the years, being uniquely well-equipped for the purpose.

On 9 July 1956 Lord Templewood, a former Conservative Home Secretary, by that time President of the Howard League for Penal Reform, rose to move the Second Reading of the Death Penalty (Abolition) Bill. 'I am here today,' said Lord Templewood, 'to ask for the Second Reading of a Bill that has gone through all its stages in another place. It is sponsored by a private Member who, in the face of admitted Government opposition, has managed to get this Bill passed through all its stages.'

Lord Templewood recalled that he had made 'a not dissimilar speech' in 1948 when the side that he supported was defeated by 181 votes to 28. 'But since then,' he argued, 'great changes have come about.' He cited in particular the evidence placed before the Royal Commission which had reported in the meanwhile. He drew to a close by stating five propositions. 'First, that the present law is admittedly unsatisfactory; secondly, that the death penalty is not an essential deterrent; thirdly, that an execution is a horrible proceeding; fourthly, that life imprisonment is an equally effective deterrent; fifthly, that the death penalty, being irrevocable, makes mistakes irremediable.' The Lord Chancellor, Lord Kilmuir, stated straight-away the views of the government. 'Her Majesty's Government,' he said, 'are clearly and unequivocally of the view that capital punishment must be retained. I apprehend,' he went on, 'that to most of your Lordships, the real crux of the question at issue in this debate is whether capital punishment is in effect a uniquely effective deterrent.' He was obviously satisfied of that in spite of all the evidence that had been assembled against that point of view, the opinion that capital punishment was a unique deterrent was still overwhelmingly strong.

Lord Pethick Lawrence, speaking first from the Labour front bench, called attention to the constitutional issue: 'We have a constitutional issue – an unusual thing. I do not ever remember in the course of my life the carrying by another place, through all its stages, of a Bill which was from the start opposed by the government of the day. Noble Lords in all parts of the House recognise the fact that we may be faced with a constitutional issue between this House and another place.' He then proceeded to spell out the recognised arguments for abolition. Over 60 speakers took part. Only a few of them can be mentioned here. The Archbishop of York surprisingly went out of his way to denounce Christian Action for encouraging the public to what he called 'superficial thinking in favour of abolition'. Nevertheless, he concluded 'it is what I will call the concomitants and atmosphere surrounding the place of the death penalty in the nation, that have come to weigh with me and to lead me to the conclusion – a conclusion reached by balancing the two views, each of which has moral potency attached to it – that it will be for the good of this country if this Bill passes your Lordships' House and becomes law.'

Lord Hailsham, many years later to become Lord Chancellor after a period of return to the Commons, was if possible even more resolute on the other side. 'In my mind the conclusive argument is that if this Bill becomes law we shall have a situation in which there will be a certain number of murders where there will be no deterrence from murder at all or where the additional deterrent is only marginal. I am compelled to say that I regard the burden of proof as upon those who wish to bring about that situation.' Their case had not been made out. The Lord Chief Justice, Lord Goddard, was always listened to with exceptional, almost morbid, interest on such matters. He did not disappoint this time. 'I still believe,' said he, 'that a man who deliberately murdered another has committed the supreme crime and should pay the supreme penalty.' I can still hear the passion with which he described a certain crime and delivered the verdict. 'Such a man should be destroyed.' When it came to the vote those who supported the Bill were 95, those who opposed 238. The total voting of 333 was far larger than at any time in my experience until then.

But the abolitionists were not done with yet, nor was the House of Commons. By February 1957 we find the same Lord Chancellor, Lord Kilmuir, introducing a Homicide Bill which represented a compromise between the abolitionists and the so-called retentionists. In other words it restricted capital punishment to certain categories of murder. He put the best face on it that he could. 'The Government's opinion,' he said, 'is already known that the retention of capital punishment is necessary in some cases to safeguard law and order. That principle,' he insisted, 'is preserved by this Bill but we have thought it right to go a long way to meet the views of those who are opposed to the application of capital punishment under the present law.' Lord Silkin was somewhat derisory of the reasons for the introduction of the Bill. 'There can be no reasonable doubt that this Bill comes before your Lordships at this time and with this haste not merely or solely out of a passionate desire to reform the criminal law. It comes, in my view and in the view of a good many of us, from a desire to anticipate the operation of the Parliament Act, which would have operated if a Bill similar to the Silverman Bill had been allowed to go through another place and had passed.' Whatever the motivation this so-called Compromise Bill passed into law without much difficulty.

But the movement for abolition continued to gather strength. To the best of my recollection, every Labour MP returned to Parliament in 1964 was in favour of it, many of them passionately so, although in the Labour Party, as in the other parties, it was rightly treated as a matter of private conscience. It was inevitable that, when Labour came back to power in autumn 1964, a strong attempt would be made to abolish capital punishment. There was, of course, much support outside that particular party.

On 19 July 1965, Baroness Wootton of Abinger moved that the Murder (Abolition of Death Penalty) Bill be read a second time. It had already been passed by the House of Commons by a majority of 2 to 1. Baroness Wootton was something of a phenomenon in the post-war House in more ways than one. She was one of the first four women to take their seats in the House under the Life Peerages Act of 1958.

When she was an undergraduate at Cambridge Barbara Wootton had obtained a first-class degree in economics with a special asterisk, I like to think the first and last of its kind. Her academic distinctions were numerous but in recent years she had become best known as a criminologist. Any disposition on the part of the Conservatives to treat her as a mere intellectual was countered by the fact that she had served as a magistrate for over 30 years. A fine-looking woman with impressive white hair and stylish spectacles. She was a formidable figure but soon much loved in the House.

I need not recapitulate the arguments which she was particularly well qualified to propound. The two last Conservative Lord Chancellors, Lord Dilhorne and Lord Kilmuir, maintained their resolute opposition but the bishops and archbishops, who had voted for abolition as long ago as 1956, were among the many peers who supported it now. The Lord Chancellor on this occasion was Lord Gardiner, who had probably done more than any individual for the abolitionist cause. Very significant was the speech of the Lord Chief

Justice, Lord Parker. Very different indeed from that of the previous Lord Chief Justice, Lord Goddard, in 1956.

He asked the House to realise 'that all the judges are quite disgusted at the results produced by the Homicide Act.' He referred to the complete absurdities and inconsistencies that emerged. He would vote for the Second Reading of this Bill, subject to certain safeguards. When it came to the vote those who were Content with the Bill numbered 204, those Not Content, 104. This was roughly the same majority as in the House of Commons. The retentionists continued the struggle. One or two amendments were introduced and accepted by the government including one which most penal reformers today regard as unfortunate. It gives a power to the judges in passing a life sentence to make a recommendation as to how long the prisoner should serve. But in essentials the Bill was carried as introduced. It should be mentioned that it should initially run for five years only. To become permanent it would require an affirmative resolution of both Houses which in the event was forthcoming.

On the Third Reading Lords Dilhorne and Kilmuir had repeated their opposition. The Lord Chief Justice, Lord Parker, had repeated his support, informing the House that almost all the judges agreed with him. Lord Gardiner's final speech was particularly moving to those who knew that it represented so many years of selfless endeavour. In the event the House divided. Contents 169, Not Contents 75. Many distinguished Conservatives were among the Contents. Lord Carrington, a recent Leader of the House, and Lady Elliott, one of the first women peers along with Lady Wootton, among them. The bishops as consistently as during the previous 10 years were in favour, as was the Lord Chief Justice, but his predecessor Lord Goddard, and Lord Chancellor Dilhorne were not surprisingly in the opposite lobby.

It must not be thought that the House of Lords has been reactionary on penal matters generally. I myself opened a debate on prisons in 1955 which was at that time without precedent. Since then I have taken part in many debates and initiated not a few on matters of this kind. But in recent years the outstanding performers have been Lord Donaldson, President of NACRO, Lord Hunt, at one time the Chairman of the Parole Board, Lord Hutchinson, a former leader of the Criminal Bar, and Lord Harris of Greenwich, a former Minister of State at the Home Office and like Lord Hunt a former Chairman of the Parole Board. Lord Windlesham, also a former minister of state at the Home Office and still, at the time of writing, Chairman of the Parole Board, has written a first class description of penal policy from the Conservative standpoint. In recent times much authority has been lent to the cause of penal reform by Lord Elwyn-Jones, Lord Mishcon and Lord Graham of Edmonton, who speaks officially for the prison officers. There is no doubt that our penal team in the Lords is much stronger than anything that has ever been produced in the Commons, though Robert Kilroy Silk while he was an MP rendered yeoman service.

Homosexuality

In the case of homosexuality, a combination of influences was at work. In 1956 a government-appointed committee, chaired by Lord Wolfenden, issued a report on homosexuality and prostitution. I will pass over the second part of their mandate. In fact their proposals were followed up not long afterwards by a Bill to limit prostitution in public. It was with the first part, male homosexuality (in those days we hardly seemed to be aware of lesbianism) with which I was mainly concerned when I opened a debate in the House of Lords on 4 December 1957. Lord Boothby described me as 'the non-playing captain of the homosexual team' which I took as a kind of compliment. It may be asked, however, why I took the lead on this matter when it was thought in the House of Commons to be far too hot a potato to handle. Accident, I suppose, came in here.

I had been very much involved with penal matters in the preceding two years. I was at that time visiting all the leading prisons and borstals in the course of an enquiry for the Nuffield Foundation into the causes of crime (later published as a book). In company with

197

several friends during this period I founded the New Bridge for Ex-Prisoners, a society which still flourishes today. In the course of all this I became friendly with three gifted young men of social standing who had been serving sentences for secondary homosexual offences. Indeed, the Home Office were supposed to be saying that our society, the New Bridge, was a gang of homosexuals helping other homosexuals. (When it was pointed out to them that at that time I had eight children they are supposed to have said 'Oh, that's just cover'.) Be that as it may, I became profoundly concerned about the plight of homosexuals in general, most of whom would have far fewer friends than the ones I have mentioned. Hence my fervent adoption of the main principle, then highly controversial, of the Wolfenden report. According to the Wolfenden proposal it would no longer be a criminal offence to have sex with a consenting male over 21 in private.

In my speech of introduction I talked specifically in a Christian sense though not representing anyone but myself. I enunciated as my guidelines the formula that I have used so often since. We must hate the sin and love the sinner. I proceeded from that starting-point to arrive at the same conclusion as the Wolfenden Committee.

The great majority of those who spoke supported my submission. This is not an infallible clue in the House of Lords because those who support a cause are more likely to speak than those who don't. But men of great distinction took up varying positions. The Archbishop of Canterbury agreed with the Wolfenden proposal, so did the Bishop of St. Albans, speaking on behalf of the Church of England Moral Welfare Council. On the other hand the Bishop of Carlisle insisted that if ever any government dealt with this problem in this way it would be a 'terrible thing'. The Bishop of Rochester spoke still more strongly in the same sense. 'If your Lordships had known the problem we had in Chatham during the War when men came down in great numbers to sleuth [sic] young naval ratings, you would know that we have a responsibility to protect people from this kind of corrupting menace.'

The Lord Chancellor, Lord Kilmuir, was ready to describe the report as a great landmark and to show considerable sympathy for the proposals regarding prostitution but as regards homosexuality he disappointed the reformers. 'Even,' he said, 'if it were thought right to accept the committee's recommendations in principle, and Her Majesty's Government will not think that, very difficult consequential problems would arise.' He did not believe that at the present time 'the general sense of the community was with the Committee in the recommendations.' He made it plain that there was no prospect of early legislation of that kind.

Lord Denning, a Lord of Appeal in Ordinary 1957–62 (after much deliberation he told me later), came down decisively against Wolfenden. 'Is this conduct,' he asked, 'so wrongful and so harmful that in the opinion of Parliament it should be publicly condemned and in proper cases punished? I would say that the answer was "yes".' There was no division, the motion being, in accordance with the usual practice, withdrawn. The House of Lords had rushed in where angels, in the form of the House of Commons, had feared to tread. But the Law was strongly opposed to reform, the Church somewhat but not entirely favourable. There was certainly no prospect, as the Lord Chancellor said, of early legislation.

We move on to 1965 when Lord Arran introduced a Bill to give effect to the Wolfenden principle explained above. The Lord Arran of the day was a Conservative peer of highly individual flavour, possessed of the rapid speech and nervous gestures of his Cecil relatives, much also of their brilliance. By this time, ten years after Wolfenden, the great majority of the House were favourable to change.

When the Third Reading was voted on the Contents were 83, the Not Contents, 49. Lord Arran had conducted proceedings with much skill and wit but the most famous intervention came from Field Marshal Lord Montgomery. The Bill, in accordance with Wolfenden, was making it legal to have sex in private with a consenting adult over 21. Lord Montgomery moved an amendment to alter 21 to 80. He explained that he had already attained that age and he could assure the House that no one was dangerous or endangered after that age. 'After the age of 80 it does not really matter what we do.'

Lord Arran's Bill was not followed up in the Commons. A similar Bill was introduced and carried through both Houses without much difficulty in 1967. It could fairly be claimed that the House of Lords had for good or for ill given a lead to the other place. I had had no difficulty in supporting Lord Arran's Bill and the subsequent legislation. But a decade later he seemed to me to be pushing his luck too far. Lord Arran now wished to lower the age of consent from 21 to 18. He introduced a Bill to that effect on 14 June 1977. He made the plausible point that the Wolfenden Committee had proposed the age of 21 because, in their words, 'All things considered, the legal age of contractual responsibility seemed to us to afford the best criterion for the definition of adulthood in this respect.' Since then the legal age of majority had been lowered to 18, hence on Wolfenden principles, the legal age of consent for homosexual acts should be 18 also. Lord Halsbury led the opposition. Lord Halsbury, outstanding as a Christian and a scientist, though certainly not a Christian Scientist, spoke with much power. His amendment, which in fact negated the Bill, summed up the contents of his speech. 'In view of the growth in activities of groups and individuals exploiting male prostitution and its attendant corruption of youth, debasement of morals and spread of venereal disease, this House declines to give the Bill a Second Reading.'

I myself, with some heart-searching, supported him, though less ferociously. I did not retract my initiation of the debate in 1956. The real question, I asked, was whether if the present Bill were carried, young men of 18, 19 and 20 would have a better chance of leading a good and happy life than at present. I concluded that far more were likely to be damaged than benefited. In the event Lord Arran's proposal was overwhelmingly defeated by 146 votes to 25.

One final debate which related to homosexuality must be referred to. On 18 December 1986 Lord Halsbury introduced a Bill which prevented a local authority from giving financial or other assistance to any person for the purpose of publishing or promoting homosexuality as an acceptable family relationship or for the purpose of teaching such acceptability in any school. Here again I supported Lord Halsbury, though once again after considerable heart-searching. Lord Halsbury made much play with some admittedly outrageous documents emerging from what he called the loony left local authorities. I descended into levity with something of a serious purpose. 'I am bound to say that when I hear these references to the loony left from the noble Earl, whom I am supporting, my mind goes back to the great school – he now regards it as the greatest of schools – which we both attended [Eton]. He was there rather later than I, but we overlapped. I think that from our experience of that great school (and the other public schoolboys who may be present today may agree) in those days at least homosexuality was not a perquisite of the working class. I think that is something to be borne in mind because old public schoolboys may become a little self righteous and they may be asked: where do the ideas of the "loony left" come from?' By December 1986 all except blind partisans of the Labour Party were unhappy about a good deal of the material emanating from some of the local authorities. Speaking from the Labour benches, though not in these latter days from the front bench, I tried to steer a middle course, possibly pleasing no one.

Lord Halsbury's Bill passed through all its stages in the House of Lords without difficulty but time was not found for it in the House of Commons with an election in the offing. Amendments, with the approval of the government, to the Local Government Bill of 1987/88 implemented much of Lord Halsbury's Bill. They aroused intense opposition especially in literary and artistic circles but were carried successfully through the House.

Abortion

There is a certain parallel between the initiatives taken by, or at any rate through, the House of Lords in regard to homosexuality and abortion law reform.

In the latter case however the true initiative came from the Abortion Law Reform Society who had laboured on behalf of their cause for many years. On 25 November 1965 Lord Silkin introduced a Bill calling for abortion law reform, a subject at that time new to the House. Not many of us outside his circle realised that there would be a vote at the end of the day. When a vote took place a few of us went into the No Lobby but we were heavily out-voted by 70 to 8. Lord Barrington came up to me afterwards and asked me, dropping his voice, 'Is this a Catholic thing or are heretics allowed to join in?' In fact, of the opponents of the resolution, seven were Catholics and one was married to a Catholic. On receiving a fervent welcome from me, Lord Barrington got going. The Society for the Preservation of the Unborn Child was born and set to work very late in the day to counter the highly efficient propaganda of the Abortion Law Reform Society.

The crucial element in the triumph of Abortion Law Reform in 1966/67 was the presence of Roy Jenkins (now Lord Jenkins) as Home Secretary. The story has been told at considerable length elsewhere by supporters of the reform. To retell it briefly, Roy Jenkins gave every encouragement to David Steel, who introduced the measure that was eventually passed into law in the summer of 1967. Meanwhile, Lord Silkin had struck out boldly for the same cause in the House of Lords following his original success. A Bill introduced by him was passed by the House of Lords early in 1966 but fell to the ground owing to the General Election. The whole issue was then taken over by the House of Commons. Mr Steel's Bill was carried through that House.

As a member of the Cabinet at the time I was well aware that the great majority of the Cabinet were favourable to this Bill, although, as it emanated from a private member, we were free to vote as we chose in either House. The government provided the facilities in the House of Commons so necessary for the success of a private member's measure.

The Second Reading of the Abortion Bill was moved in the Lords on 19 July 1967 by the gallant Lord Silkin. The Bill was carried overwhelmingly by 127 votes to 21. I myself was in an unusual position as Leader of the House of disagreeing with the great majority of my colleagues. I took a step unprecedented in my time of leaving my seat on the middle of the front bench and speaking against it from a back bench. If it had been a Government Bill I would of course have felt it a duty to resign. The arguments for and against this far-reaching reform need not be recited here. A high proportion of the 21 who opposed the Bill were Roman Catholics, though we included in our ranks the Bishop of Exeter. Three bishops however voted with the great majority. The Bill eventually became the law under which at the time of writing we are still living.

The Government, as I say, were not officially committed to either side but their warm support for the Bill was well known. Lord Stonham, Parliamentary Under-Secretary at the Home Office, voted in favour of the Bill.

Nineteen years on (28 January 1987), the Bishop of Birmingham introduced a Bill which was generally felt to be a slight amendment of the Abortion Act, though he himself said, 'This Bill is not about the Abortion Act at all. It is about infant life preservation and, in particular about the act of 1929 which bears that name. My Bill,' he said, 'has one moral pre-supposition and one only and it is this. It is immoral and wrong to kill a child capable of being born alive.' Since the Abortion Act of 1967 the forces of opposition who had been taken by surprise at that time had built up considerable strength and found large numbers of men and women who were critical of the Act. There were many who had supported it who felt that abortion on demand, which had been strenuously disclaimed at the time, had come close to being a reality. All attempts however to amend the Bill and, in practice, to restrict the number of abortions had been defeated, that is to say counted out in the House of Commons, even when a majority in favour of them seemed to exist. No government had taken the step which was taken by the Labour Government in 1967 of making unlimited time available.

The Bishop of Birmingham, shortly about to retire after notable service in the House of Lords, informed the House that he introduced this Bill with some reluctance and a great deal of trepidation. 'It is a long time since a Bishop introduced a Bill in your Lordships' House' – a point that was not without interest. The arguments flowed backwards and forwards. The doughty 89-year-old Lord Houghton, much concerned with the original reform of the law, argued vehemently against the measure. The Government spokesman, Lord Beaverbrook, grandson of the founder of the line, surprised and pleased supporters of the Bill by announcing unequivocally at the end of his speech 'I commend this measure to your Lordships' House.' The vote however was taken late at night, 13 minutes past 11; it was a close finish, no one can say what would have occurred with a full attendance. In the end 41 voted for the Bill, 31 against. Nearly a third of the supporters of the Bill were Roman Catholics but they were balanced by some long-term humanists, led by Lord Houghton. The Bill was ultimately killed by the coming of the General Election. The Lords may be thought to have been more critical of abortion in 1987 than in 1967 but it would be hard to be dogmatic. By the time this book is published, it should be easier to form an opinion. Much may have happened in the meanwhile. The indomitable Lord Houghton neither slumbers nor sleeps.

Pornography

The House of Lords in recent years has been unequivocally hostile to pornography. By and large the House of Commons, though not favourable to it, has been less vociferous. The Christian front or Christian lobby, or whatever one chooses to call it, has been well to the fore in the Lords. As already mentioned, Lords Nugent, Halsbury, Ingleby and Robertson have been prominent but so have a number of others.

The successful restriction on indecent display by sex shops of video nasties and the use of children in pornographic production – in all these matters the Lords have played a crucial part.

I cannot without affectation fail to mention our first debate on pornography which I initiated in April 1971. It led to the setting up of a committee whose report was debated in the House of Lords in November 1972 on the initiative of the then Bishop of Leicester, Chairman of the Church of England Board of Social Responsibility. In each case a large majority of the speakers supported the general assault on pornography launched by myself and the Bishop. Too much must not be read into that. As mentioned earlier, the participants in these general debates tend to sympathise with the proposer of a motion. Nevertheless, then and in the subsequent 15 years, I have been conscious of a very powerful dislike of pornography in the House of Lords.

In opening the debate of 21 April 1971, I laid down some propositions which may seem obvious but will bear repetition. I started from the assumption that we all dislike pornography but we also dislike censorship. The question was how to overcome the first without falling a victim to the second. We all probably agreed that a line had to be drawn somewhere, the question was where should that line be drawn in terms of the criminal law? I conceded that it was extraordinarily difficult to prove that any particular piece of pornography was damaging to morals but I submitted without hesitation the proposition that 'a diet of filth corrupts the nation'. 'Pornography,' I stated with equal confidence, 'has increased, is increasing and ought to be diminished.'

Nineteen months later the Bishop of Leicester, who had been one of the leading Members of the committee in the meanwhile, justified the general lines of our report. Neither he nor I nor any member of the committee would have claimed that the detailed recommendations we made were the only ones which would serve the agreed purpose of curbing pornography.

Ten years later on 25 March 1982 Lord Nugent of Guildford moved the Second Reading of his Private Members' Bill intended to prevent the dissemination of pornography. He made a number of points more effectively than I had done on earlier occasions. I referred to him and Lord Halsbury as the Castor and Pollux of the battle against pornography.

'It is a matter of tremendous joy,' I said, 'that the torch which dropped from my palsied hands ten years ago has been grabbed by these fresh virile young figures.' (They were both considerably younger than me but neither would see 70 again!)

Lord Nugent deliberately confined himself to 'hard pornography'. He conceded more than I would have done in announcing: 'public opinion is prepared to tolerate "soft pornography" even if many do not like it.' The point at which pornography became objectionable to most people, and therefore definable as hard pornography, would vary from one decade to another, and much which would have been judged intolerable 20 years ago is today judged as tolerable. Possibly in 20 years' time the pendulum might have swung back again.

'The Bill is constructed in the belief that there is a residual sludge at the bottom of the bucket which is never going to be tolerable to public opinion and should therefore be made illegal.' He had convinced himself from his discussions with the Home Secretary that nothing more ambitious than the present measure would be likely to secure sufficient governmental approval to give it a chance of becoming law.

The Disabled

There has been a marked improvement in the treatment of disabled people since 1970, a first step long overdue. In that year an epoch-making measure, the Chronically Sick and Disabled Persons Bill, passed into law. It will always be associated with the name of Alfred Morris MP, who took the vital initiative in the House of Commons and won the approval of the whole country for the proposed reforms. I was privileged in the House of Lords to introduce the Bill and take charge of it during the later stages. A certain amount of obstinacy was required in pressing amendments. The Government, though full of goodwill, were close to a general election and therefore in rather a hurry. As I was speaking on the Second Reading, a happy form of words came to me, not a very usual occurrence. 'Suffering,' I declared, 'while it sometimes degrades, can also ennoble.' My part, however, was secondary, many others could have performed it at least as well.

What gave the debate a historic character and gave the House of Lords a unique standing among the parliaments of the world was the participation of a number of Lords or Baronesses themselves disabled. Baroness Darcy de Knayth, Baroness Masham, Lord Ingleby and Lord Crawshaw all spoke from wheelchairs. Lord

Fraser of Lonsdale, known for many years as a blind champion of the blind, and Lord Wells-Pestell, who recalled that there was a long period some years ago when he was totally paralysed, should be added to the list of disabled speakers. Lord Grenfell spoke from intimate knowledge about autism and dyslexia. He had deeply moved the House on an earlier occasion by telling them about his mongol son. These speeches are all worth reading.

There is only space here to dwell on one of them. Lady Masham had been made a life peer a few years earlier. Hers was the youngest creation of a peerage in this century that I can trace. She was 34 at the time. I used to think that I was the youngest (at 39) until it was pointed out that Lord Beaverbrook had been only 37 when elevated. At any rate, Lady Masham beats all comers in this respect and, seeing that she was specifically ennobled because of her services to the disabled, it is safe to say that no one ever deserved a peerage more.

She was, at the time of a terrible hunting accident, engaged to the present Earl of Swinton. Her autobiography gives a beautiful account of his role in their marriage, of which indeed the House of Lords has caught many glimpses. She began by giving two examples of public attitudes. One an attitude of couldn't-care-less, the other full of consideration and desire to help. On travelling from Leeds to London on a very cold day she was treated with marked neglect by an attendant who failed to bring her a cup of coffee. On arrival in London she took a taxi to her destination and, when she asked the driver, who had been most helpful, what the fare was he said, 'Have this one on me.' He would accept no payment. The House was soon gripped by her description of what disablement may mean. 'I should like to stress how very much more expensive life is for the severely disabled. I myself, as a paraplegic, feel the cold; heating is an expensive item. A person wearing callipers will wear out several pairs of trousers in a year. Nearly every time I get in or out of a taxi I ladder a pair of stockings. Very often dressing is difficult, and clothes receive a great deal of wear and tear.' She proceeded to bring it home to the most insensitive of us what disablement meant in real life. She told us before she closed of a young man who had sustained a neck fracture from a truck accident. 'When he had been in a general hospital for fifteen months, I was contacted by a relative who had heard me talk on paraplegia. When I visited him I found him suffering from pressure sores and infection. Within two weeks of being transferred to a spinal injury unit this patient was feeding himself; hitherto he had not been able to do this. He had to spend a year having intensive treatment to his sores before rehabilitation could proceed. Altogether, this young man spent some 18 extra months in hospital than he need have done.'

From that debate onwards the 'armoured division' has never failed to demand the full attention of the House. It has since been added to by notable recruits in the duke of Buccleuch and Baroness Lane-Fox. In the House of Commons at the present time there are two very remarkable men, Jack Ashley who is deaf and David Blunkett who is blind. We must not seek to claim a monopoly of disabled prowess. I still maintain, however, that in this regard our House as I said earlier, is unique among the legislatures of the world.

The Committee Work of the House of Lords

The House does not commit Bills to Standing Committees, like the House of Commons, nor has it set up departmental Select Committees to keep watch on Whitehall. However, in the last 15 years it has established two important Select Committees which play major roles in the process of parliamentary scrutiny of the Executive. First, in February 1974, a year after Britain joined the European Economic Community (the 'Common Market'), the House appointed a committee to consider proposed Community legislation before British ministers agreed to it in Brussels. The committee works through six sub-committees, involving in all about 80 members of the House; it takes evidence from British ministers and Community commissioners, from trade associations and universities, and from other interested bodies from all over Europe; and it produces about

20 reports each year, many of which are debated in the House. It is said that the House of Lords looks more closely at these proposals than any other legislature in the Community. Secondly, in January 1980 the House decided to appoint a committee 'to consider Science and Technology'. The committee has been doing so ever since, under the chairmanship first of Lord Todd (a Nobel prize-winning chemist and President of the Royal Society), then from 1984 of Lord Sherfield (former ambassador to Washington and Chairman of the UK Atomic Energy Authority), and since 1987 of Lord Shackleton (former Lord privy seal and President of the Royal Geographical Society). They produce roughly two reports each year, on subjects ranging from electric vehicles to local government and from forestry to space research.

Besides these committees, the House from time to time appoints a Select Committee to consider a particular subject: the work of such a committee is finished when the Committee has made its report. Most recently, the House appointed a Select Committee on Overseas Trade in July 1983. The committee was chaired by Lord Aldington, a former minister at the Board of Trade, and its Members included former chairmen of three major nationalised industries, directors of two major banks, a former Permanent Secretary at the Foreign Office and the former Commonwealth correspondent of the *New Statesman*. The committee sat for a year, taking evidence from all sides of industry, and their report prompted a major public debate on Britain's trading prospects. Select Committees are also appointed occasionally to consider Bills which are difficult or controversial in a non-party-political way: a committee appointed in 1983 to consider two Private Members' Bills concerning charities produced as part of their report an alternative Bill which became the Charities Act 1985.

The visitor to the Committee Corridor may find himself watching a Select Committee of a different kind, where five lords sit like a bench of judges while bewigged barristers produce arguments and evidence over some very local matter, such as a right of way, or a bye-law, or a marina. This committee will be considering a 'Private Bill', whereby a private party – a company, a local authority, or even an individual – has petitioned Parliament for power to do something (for example to extend a harbour, or build a railway, or marry within the prohibited degrees of affinity) which is not possible under the general law. About 30 such Bills are promoted each year, and every one is carefully examined by both Houses of Parliament.

When objectors are not satisfied, they too can petition parliament, and put their case to a Select Committee, who may amend the Bill or reject it altogether. About six such committees sit each year; proceedings last up to a week, and often the committee will visit the locality in question. Private legislation is not covered by the parliament Act 1911, and therefore the powers of the House of Lords in this area are no less than those of the Commons. Indeed, the influence of the Lords may be somewhat greater, thanks to the system of scrutiny of 'unopposed provisions', that is those against which no objector has petitioned. The Local Government Act 1972 wiped the local statute book clean: in consequence, the last fifteen years have seen a succession of 'Jumbo' private bills, as local authorities have petitioned Parliament for the special powers which they consider their local area to require. All of these Bills have received first and most detailed consideration in the House of Lords, and one might say that the local statute book has been rewritten in the offices of the Chairman of Committees and his learned counsel.

Final Words

It is now more than 60 years since I took my first essay on Second Chambers to the Warden of New College, the famous historian H. A. L. Fisher. Later as a college tutor myself I set a similar essay year after year to my pupils. If, by some miracle, I found myself once again teaching a subject called Political Institutions, I would no doubt be asking the same questions and receiving much the same answers.

Probably in the last half century the great increase in the complexity of legislation has strengthened the case, already convincing, for a revising second chamber. Today the House of Lords seems to stand on even firmer ground. But the old problem of how to produce a defensible composition for an 'Upper House' remains as baffling as ever. Election? Direct or indirect? How to make sure that the Lower House is not unduly upstaged? A country with a federal constitution offers possibilities not available to a unitary state like Britain.

Appointment by the Executive? But how to avoid undue patronage falling into the hands of the Prime Minister or equivalent leader? One thing can be stated with certainty. No one, at any date, if they were providing a second chamber for a newly formed state, would take the British House of Lords as a model. It has not had and is not likely to have imitators.

Yet the hereditary principle, the most distinctive feature of the House of Lords, shows no sign of being superseded. There was one moment (see Chapter X) when the right of hereditary peers to vote in the Chamber seemed likely to be extinguished. I have explained above the circumstances which defeated that initiative. There are no present signs of its being repeated.

If the Labour Party came into power with a large majority such as that of 1945, it is possible that the hereditary principle in the House of Lords would be assaulted in earnest. That is for the future. It was significant that in 1987, for the first time for many years, the Labour Party Election Manifesto made no reference to reform, drastic or otherwise, of the House of Lords. We must take the House therefore as we find it with its strange amalgam of hereditary peers, former members of the House of Commons, bishops, law lords and experts of every conceivable variety.

Enoch Powell in his scholarly work on the House of Lords in the Middle Ages has offered this arresting opinion: 'Few institutions have retained their identity so long and through so many political and social revolutions as the English House of Lords.' I do not see matters quite like that, though Mr Powell calls attention to an important aspect. The House in which I have served for 43 years is 'changed utterly' from the House of the Middle Ages where the spiritual lords predominated, from the House of 1641 which made Strafford kneel before them and later condemned him to death, or the House of 1893 which voted down the second Home Rule Bill, already passed by the Commons, by 419 votes to 41. Yet the ritual, as illustrated in the Prelude, preserves many unchanging features. The House remains the only assembly known to me which is so much a master of its own affairs that it permits no chairman to control its business.

The many changes that have taken place over the centuries have been carried out within a framework of accepted procedures. As I said at the beginning of this book, all who work in the House, the Peers and the devoted staff, are conscious of a continuous tradition which began long before them and must be expected to maintain itself long after their time.

Lord Bryce wound up his *History of the Holy Roman Empire* with this fine peroration: 'Its place in human history it can never lose. Into it all the life of the ancient world was gathered. Out of it all the life of the modern world arose.'

I will not attempt so grandiloquent a eulogy of the House of Lords. But I submit with confidence that it will never lose its place in British history, that its record is inextricably bound up with that of the nation and that its significance in its endless evolution is not likely to diminish in the years to come.

End Note

The House of Lords moves on waiting for no one, least of all the putative historian. The text of this book was virtually completed by the end of 1987. Since then the House of Lords has been more consistently in the news than at any time in my experience. Three Government measures have aroused intense controversy: Clause 28, prohibiting local authorities from propaganda deemed to favour homosexuality, a massive Bill for educational reform and a Bill, equally massive, for transferring the burden of the rates from property to persons. The debate on all three measures have been exceptionally well-informed and strenuous. At the time of writing (end of May 1988) it does not seem that the assessment of the House of Lords today, submitted in Chapter XI, needs qualification.

Four votes in particular may be taken to illustrate the underlying realities. On the Bill for Educational Reform the Government was defeated twice at the Committee stage. They were beaten by 141 votes to 122 on the method of 'opting out' and by 152 to 126 on academic freedom. An Opposition amendment, however, resisting the abolition of the Inner London Education Authority was defeated by 236 votes to 183. The liability of the government in a part-time House to be defeated on a number of occasions, but to prevail when they pull out all the stops was demonstrated once again. The decisiveness of their reserve power was made still more evident when an amendment to the Poll Tax proposal moved by a popular Conservative back-bencher and supported in the Division Lobby by three former Cabinet ministers was defeated by 317 votes to 183. The total size of this vote has only once been exceeded.

The vote on entry into the EEC on 28 October 1971 produced 451 Contents, 58 Not Contents, a total of 509 compared with the vote of 500 on the Poll Tax amendment. Old-timers like myself were not much surprised. But the size of the majority came as a shock to many inside and outside the House.

Certain changes which have occurred since the end of 1987 must be noted. The Social Democratic party in the House, as outside it, has partitioned itself. At the time of writing 19 of the Social Democratic peers have joined the Liberals to form the SLD party of 61 members. Lord Jenkins of Hillhead, a former Home Secretary and Chancellor of the Exchequer, has become their leader. Baroness Seear, who led the Liberals previously, remains a vigorous presence. So does Lord Diamond who previously led the Social Democrats. He hands over to Baroness Stedman, formerly Chief Whip, who now leads a party of 25. She reminds me that there were only nine of them to begin with. Lord Whitelaw, to general regret, was compelled by ill-health to resign the Leadership of the House. He has handed it over to Lord Belstead, a trusted servant of the House.

The House has recently been enriched by the arrival of a number of leading ex-Cabinet ministers and of some ardent spirits from a younger school.

Select Bibliography

Bagehot, Walter, *The English Constitution*, London 1867 (revised 1872)

Beckett, J. V., *The Aristocracy in England 1660–1914*, (Oxford 1986)

Blakiston, Georgiana, *Woburn and the Russells*, (London 1980)

Bond, Maurice, (ed) *Works of Art in the House of Lords*, HM Stationery Office, 1980

Brock, Michael, *The Great Reform Act* (London 1973)

Brown, A. L., 'Parliament, *c.* 1377–1422' in *The English Parliament in the Middle Ages* eds. R. G. Davies and J. M. Denton (Manchester 1981), pp. 109–140

Bryce, James, Viscount, *The Holy Roman Empire*, (Oxford 1864)

Cecil, Lord David, *The Cecils of Hatfield House*, (London 1973)

Cooke, Sir Robert, *The Palace of Westminster*, (London 1987)

Cormack, Patrick, M.P., *Westminster Palace and Parliament*, (London 1981)

Elton, G. R., *The Parliament of England 1559–1581*, (Cambridge 1986)

Firth, C. M., *The House of Lords during the Civil War*, (London 1910)

Fox, Alice, W., *The Earl of Halsbury, Lord High Chancellor, 1823–1921*, (London 1929)

Fraser, Antonia, *King Charles II*, (London 1979)

Fulford, Roger, *The Trial of Queen Caroline*, (London 1967)

Graves, M. A. R., *The House of Lords in the Parliaments of Edward VI and Mary I: an Institutional Study*, (London 1981)

Harriss, G. L, 'The Formation of Parliament, 1272–1377' in *The English Parliament in the Middle Ages*, eds. R. G. Davies and J. H. Denton, (Manchester 1981), pp. 29–60

Holmes, Geoffrey, *British Politics in the Age of Anne*, (London 1985)

Jenkins, Roy, *Mr Balfour's Poodle*, (London 1954)

Jones, Christopher, *The Great Palace*, (London 1983)

Lacey, Robert, *Aristocrats*, (London 1983)

Minney, R. J., *Viscount Addison: Leader of the Lords*, (London 1958)

Morgan, Janet, *The House of Lords and the Labour Government 1964–1970*, (Oxford 1975)

Newton, Lord, *Lord Lansdowne, a Biography*, (London 1929)

Ogg, David, *England in the Reign of James II and William III*, (Oxford 1955)

Pike, Luke Owen, *The Constitutional History of the House of Lords*, (London 1894)

Pollard, A. F., *The Evolution of Parliament*, (London 1920)

Powell, Enoch, *The House of Lords in the Middle Ages*, (London 1968)

Read-Foster, Elizabeth, *The House of Lords 1603–1949*, (London 1983)

Russell, Conrad, *Parliaments and English Politics 1621–1629*, (Oxford 1979)

Robinson, John Martin, *The Dukes of Norfolk*, (Oxford 1982)

Rose, Kenneth, *The Later Cecils*, (London 1975)

Stevens, Robert, *Law and Politics – the House of Lords as a Judicial Body*, (Chapel Hill 1979)

Trevor-Roper, Hugh, *The Life of Archbishop Laud*, (London 1940)

Turbeville, A. S., 'The House of Lords and the Reform Act of 1832' in *Proceedings of the Leeds Philosophical and Literary Society, Literary and Historical Section*, 6, (1945), pp. 61–92

Tunstall, Brian, *William Pitt, Earl of Chatham*, (London 1938)

Wagner, Anthony and Sainty, J. C., 'The origin of the introduction of Peers in the House of Lords', *Archaeologia*, ci, (1976), pp. 119–150

Wiffen, J. H., *Historical memoirs of the House of Russell*, (London 1833)

Index

INDEX

INDEX